PEACE AND LOVE ALWAYS !

May Harrison

PROV. 16:3

WINGS OF FAITH

May the wings of faith uphold you
When your cross is hard to bear,
As temptations surround you,
And no one seems to care.

May the wings of faith surround you
And shield you from the pain
When sorrows overcome you
And teardrops fall like rain.

May you know that God is with you
In times of deep despair.
May the spirit, who's within you,
Confirm that He is there!

May the valley of the shadow
Provide angels unaware...
May the wings of faith uphold you
When your cross is hard to bear.

Poet, Clay Harrison

BY CLAY HARRISON

DEDICATION

I thank God for the gift of poetry. I have always felt His presence on my spiritual journey through life.

I thank God for my wife, Shirley, who has stood by and inspired me through 51 years of marriage. She has spent countless hours on the computer editing and cropping photographs for this memoir.

I thank my children, grandchildren, the pastors, nuns and friends mentioned in this book for always being there for me. I am richly blessed!

FORWARD

I am living proof that miracles still happen, God is still in control of His creation, and we can rise above our problems on the wings of faith.

Our prayers may not be answered as we would like them to be but they will be answered, in time, according to God's will. I survived a 35 year career in law enforcement and a heart attack. My wife is a 12 year breast cancer survivor.

At age 16, I received the gift of poetry and for 60 years I have written poems to encourage others and honor God. Faith and hope are central themes throughout my poetry. I was born in poverty, but I have met and written poems for some very famous people.
May you be richly blessed!

Clay Harrison

WINGS OF FAITH

ACKNOWLEDGEMENTS

The author wishes to express his gratitude to the following publishers for their encouragement and their permission to reprint these poems:
Ideals Publications,
Salesian Inspirational Books,
June Cotner Publications,
Saturday Evening Post,
Woman's World magazine,
Editor's Desk,
Jean's Journal,
The Moccasin,
Quill and Scroll,
Rhyme Time,
Love Letters,
The Pegasus Review,
The Creative Urge,
Poets at Work,
Poetry Press,
and The Midwest Poetry Review.

WINGS OF FAITH

WINGS OF FAITH

©2018 by Clay Harrison

TABLE OF CONTENTS

WINGS OF FAITH

CHAPTER 1

CHILDHOOD MEMORIES

"Train up a child in the way he should go and when he is old, he will not depart from it." Proverbs 22:6 NIV

My journey began in Murfreesboro, Tennessee on January 27, 1942. I was born at home in a small house at the foot of a mountain. My parents, Laura Frances and Daniel Perkins Harrison had no insurance, no car, and there was no hospital nearby. My father never learned to read or write. He left school in the second grade after being stricken by scarlet fever and he never went back. He would never show any interest in "book learning."

My mother was one of eight children. She was taken out of school in the sixth grade to help on the farm. My father lived nearby. My mother learned to cook, sew, tend gardens, and was very good at making items for craft shows. Dad was fair-skinned, extremely shy and prematurely bald. He hated life on the farm and got rashes when he worked in the sun with his brothers and sisters.

I have limited knowledge of the first few years of my life because my parents never shared that part of their lives with me. I would get bits

WINGS OF FAITH

and pieces about those years later in my life while visiting my mother's parents in Tennessee, and my father's brother, Uncle Lee, when we lived in California.

For some reason, unknown to me, when I was a toddler my parents packed our meager belongings, we boarded a Greyhound bus, and settled in Tampa, Florida. Having no education or job skills caused my parents to live from payday to payday and job to job. As a result, we were constantly moving from one rented apartment to another. Our form of transportation in those days was by bus, streetcar, or walking.

We lived on the fringe of white society in the segregated south. For a time we lived above bars and pool halls on "skid row" where blood stains and vomit were common sights on the sidewalk below. One day there was a shooting below us

on Franklin Street. Flashing lights and police sirens got my attention so I wandered down the stairs to see what was happening. People were running in all directions trying to get away from a body on the sidewalk. I traipsed through the crime scene and got blood on my new shoes. When Mom found me, she was frantic. She spanked me all the way back up the stairs. Ironically, years later I would be the police officer who would walk that skid row beat.

WINGS OF FAITH

Mom and Dad took jobs usually done by "Coloreds"...janitor, dishwasher, house cleaner, elevator operator, etc. My mom was one of the first white maids in a downtown hotel. She also sewed for people; she cleaned houses and she would take me with her. At one house, someone had passed away and the body was lying on a table as the family was preparing for the wake. I was scared to death so my mom had to explain to me what was happening.

We never owned a home and my parents never had jobs that included health insurance. Since we never celebrated birthdays, I didn't know my date of birth until I started school. I did not go to Kindergarten, nor did I have any home schooling considering my parents lack of education. Mom bought my clothes from thrift stores and when I outgrew my pants, she made shorts out of them. I went barefoot most of the time and even though my feet were tough as leather, I had many cuts from stepping on sand spurs, glass, nails, etc.

I was miles behind my classmates upon entering first grade. I didn't know my A, B, C's or numbers so I was called "the dumbest kid in school" and "poor white trash." Whoever said "Sticks and stones may break my bones, but words will never hurt me" got it wrong! Ugly words hurt me deeply.

As a result of my "poor write trash" reputation, I became an outsider and a loner. I wasn't one of the popular kids except at recess. I could kick, hit, or throw a ball better than most of my classmates. I was deadly at dodge ball so I seemed to find my niche because God made me strong and fast. In my 70's now, it's the fast part I miss the most. When I became a police officer, my nickname was "the Roadrunner."

WINGS OF FAITH

CHAPTER ONE

As a child, I climbed every tree wherever we lived. High in the branches I could hide from the world and daydream and sometimes pretend I was Tarzan. But if I climbed too high, I was terrified trying to get back down. One time I climbed a tree, got up on our roof, tied a bath towel around my neck, and pretended to be Superman. I summoned up all my courage to jump off and I landed on a wire clothesline. Thankfully, the towel kept me from serious injury but needless to say, I never did that again. Lesson learned the hard way.

"POOR WHITE TRASH!"

"There ain't no shame in being poor" my mother used to say
Way back in my childhood years that seem so far away.
I often had no money and patches on my clothes,
And sometimes when I passed by, classmates would thumb their nose.
There were no birthday parties as birthdays came and went
For we would have no money to pay the next month's rent.
They may have come from thrift stores, but all my clothes were clean,
And because I played with "Coloreds," my classmates could be mean.
I did without a lot of things because I had no cash,
But the thing that hurt me most-they called me "poor white trash!"
"Sticks and stones may break my bones," but that's alright you see,
For the wounds that hurt me most were the names they called me!

During those first years in school, I struggled to catch up with the children. But I discovered that I loved learning so a whole new world opened up for me. I absorbed knowledge like a sponge but also learned how horrible racism can be. After school and on weekends, I played marbles and stickball with the neighborhood kids. At the time, we were living in a duplex apartment near the Fortune Street Bridge, and there were no playgrounds in the area.

WINGS OF FAITH

CHAPTER ONE

One day while walking by the bridge, heading for the little corner store to buy some penny candy, I saw a crowd gathering down by the river. I walked down to see what was happening, and there, hanging from the branch of a large tree, was a young black man. He was barefoot, wearing soiled jeans with no shirt; his sightless eyes wide open with a grotesque stare. His tongue was swollen and protruding from his mouth. It was a horrible sight to see. I have relived it in dreams many times through the years. The neighbors said the KKK was sending a message to blacks who dared flirt with white girls.

Living in a segregated community was confusing to me as a child. I couldn't understand why my black friends had to sit in the back of the bus and I wasn't allowed to sit with them. They could not eat at the lunch counters in the five and dime department stores; they had to order from a window outside on the sidewalk. The water fountains were marked "Colored" or "White" and I simply thought the "Colored" ones meant they had colored water. I got spanked when my mother caught me drinking from it. There were five "white" movie theaters and only one for "coloreds." I was quite surprised when I discovered that Amos and Andy on the radio were portrayed by white people pretending to be black people. It made no sense to me at all.

Life in Tampa during the 1940's and 50's was difficult for poor people. Rooms were small with no air conditioning or showers. We had iceboxes which created excitement when the iceman came by and gave the kids chips of ice. Most people had no television or telephones. Those who did have a telephone were on a "party line" which allowed the other people on the party line to listen to your conversation. Street peddlers came by now and then such as the Good Humor Ice Cream man and the Fuller Brush salesman. Trucks filled with

12

WINGS OF FAITH

watermelons came around in the summertime and you could buy a large watermelon for fifty cents. That was a real treat. There were no shopping malls and grocery stores were few and far between. To buy groceries, Mom and I rode a bus or a streetcar, and for special occasions, took a cab home when we had too much to carry.

In those days you bought live chickens which were sold from crates on pallets outside the grocery store. You picked one out, took it home, killed it, and plucked it yourself. Carrying a live chicken home on a bus was embarrassing and it annoyed the other passengers. I did not want to watch my mother behead the poor chicken. Sometimes the headless chicken would run around the yard until it died. I could never eat chicken or most other meats as a child and I still eat mostly vegetarian to this day. Mom was determined I was going to eat chicken so she made me sit at the table, crying until bedtime. Every time I took a bite, I threw up and I still do today. One day at a buffet, I thought I was getting tuna salad. It turned out to be chicken salad and I gagged at the first bite.

There was never money for an allowance so I earned my spending money by mowing lawns using a push mower like Beaver Cleaver on the TV show Leave It To Beaver. I collected discarded soda bottles around the neighborhood and redeemed them at the local "mom and pop" stores. Every neighborhood had one, usually next door to the owner's home, where they sold a variety of sundry items from milk and bread to laundry detergents and sewing accessories. Most of the stores had jars of candy which cost a penny, a cookie jar, and a pickle barrel. My neighborhood store sold sugar cane by the stalk for a nickel and I could chew on it for hours. It was also the local gossip center for the neighborhood.

CHAPTER ONE

THE LITTLE CORNER STORE

What happened to the corner stores in small town neighborhoods
Where they sold the penny candy and other sundry goods?
We collected soda bottles, returned them to the store
And thought we were wealthy then with fifty cents, or more!
We could return our comic books and swap them for some more.
We were poor, but life was good, at the little corner store.
They sold pickles from a barrel and cookies from a jar,
And it was good to have them there for we didn't have a car.
I watched "old folks" playing checkers sittin' on a crate
Until Ma called me for supper when the hour grew late.
And now that we're the "old folks," they're gone forever more.
We were poor, but life was good, at the little corner store.

Since my parents never registered to vote, there was never any talk about politics. I learned about America being involved in World War II from the newsreels at the matinee. People grew victory gardens because food was scarce and there were ration stamps for things like sugar, gasoline, and other necessities. There were also long bread lines and soup kitchens. My mother loved flowers so she created a container garden using empty Maxwell House Coffee cans. She would plant seeds or get cuttings from the neighbors. Inevitably, we would move again and her garden would go with us!

WINGS OF FAITH

CHAPTER ONE

MOM'S MAXWELL HOUSE GARDEN

In my barefoot days of summer, we never owned a home
But my mother kept a garden wherever we would roam.
She always saved her coffee cans and filled them with seeds
And we always took them with us wherever God would lead.
Work was scarce and times were bad but somehow we would cope.
Mom said if you grew flowers, that there was always hope.
Her garden brought her comfort, wherever we would go,
For somehow she felt less needy if there were seeds to sow.
We made it through the hard times according to God's plan
For Mom sowed seeds of hope in Maxwell House Coffee cans.

When I earned enough money, I would go to the Saturday matinee where for several hours, I could pretend to ride the Wild, Wild West with my six-gun heroes. I loved Roy Rogers...I wanted to be Roy Rogers!Every year I asked the five and dime Santa for a Roy Rogers Cowboy Suit, complete with cap guns and hat. Every year I got marbles, Duncan yo-yo's, plastic cowboys and Indians, and a stocking filled with tangerines, mixed nuts, and candy canes. When I was eight, the miracle happened! I got my Roy Rogers Cowboy Suit, complete with cap guns and hat. My mother cried to see me so happy but it would be many years before I learned that she had hocked her wedding band to buy me that suit.

15

CHAPTER ONE

WHEN I WAS SIX OR EIGHT

I thought that death was make-believe when I was six or eight,
Perhaps some game that grownups play or they're just sleeping late.
I watched my six-gun heroes shoot the "bad guys" every week
In the early nineteen fifties when westerns hit their peak.
There was magic in those six-guns that shot ten times or more
Before the "bad guys" hit the dust just like the week before.
I never knew someone who died so how could I relate?
I thought that death was make-believe when I was six or eight.
Then came the war in Vietnam and I was called away
Where death was real and young men died in battle every day.
Here there was no make believe, no toy guns shooting caps,
There were only flag-draped coffins and buglers blowing Taps.

THOSE SATURDAY MATINEE'S

Saturday was a special day when I was a kid.
I'd hurry to the matinee to see what Hoppy did.
I'd fill up on penny candy, and get a hot dog for a dime.
Each hero was a dandy; I had a real good time.
First they'd show six cartoons, like "Casper the Friendly Ghost,"
But Bugs and those Looney Tunes tickled me the most.
Then came the weekly serial..."Would Flash Gordon get away?"
I never missed a single reel; I lived for Saturday!
I loved each double feature...Red Rider rides again.
Abbott and Costello met a creature...I just had to grin.
Tarzan swung from tree to tree; Sabu could ride a tiger.
Dracula scared "it" out of me; my eyes would grow wider.
When Roy Rogers rode the West, I knew there would be action.
My heart pounded in my chest; movies brought such satisfaction.
I remember well the Durango Kid; I cheered for Lash LaRue.
I marveled at the things they did that I could never do.
Rex, Tex, and Gene Autry could sing; Joel McCrea could surely ride.

WINGS OF FAITH

CHAPTER ONE

Movies were my favorite thing; I laughed until I cried.
Movies then were wholesome, rated for the family.
Just look how far we've come, since movies were rated "G."
Those days are gone forever, but I never will forget
When heroes ruled the matinee and rode off into the sunset.

Sometimes the cowboy stars would make personal appearances between movies at the matinee and they would give away autographed photos. This was a real treat for all of us lucky enough to be there on that day. Once, the Duncan Yo-Yo Company sponsored a contest at the matinee and every kid received a yo-yo. Those who were able to perform the most tricks such as "walkin' the dog," "around the world," etc. went home with a brand new bicycle! I wished the competition was a marble shooting contest so I could have won that brand new bicycle.

When I was in the fifth grade, my teacher was showing an after school short movie, "A Man Without A Country." It cost twenty-five cents and we needed a permission slip to stay after school to see it. I was the only kid in class who got neither. So, I decided I would sneak a peek by climbing up the fire escape to the second floor classroom where I could peek through the window. Naturally, I got caught. The teacher saw me, called my mother, and I got punished.

Mom's chosen way of rendering discipline was "switching." She would cut a small branch from the nearest tree and strike my backside and legs with it. Many times that drew blood on my skinny bare legs. Now that is called child abuse. I often prayed that our next home would be treeless so she wouldn't be able to do that to me. I wasn't a disobedient child, but I always seemed to be getting in trouble. I was either late for supper; I got my clothes dirty playing marbles, etc.

17

WINGS OF FAITH

CHAPTER ONE

My father punished me only once when Mom insisted that he spank me with a belt for showing disrespect and "sassing" her. He didn't want to do it but Mom was always the boss around the house so he was afraid not to do it. When I started to cry, he cried too. He put down the belt and never hit me again.

I seemed to get in more trouble by accident than most kids do on purpose. I knew how much my mother loved yellow flowers so one day when I saw some pretty yellow flowers blooming on the side of the road, I decided to surprise her with a bouquet. I was the one who got surprised. How was I to know they were prickly pears! Mom was not happy having to pluck dozens of spines from my hands with her tweezers and neither was I.Once, when my father made my mom really angry, she chased him through the house snapping at his bald head with a wet dish towel. He really hated that! On a full run, Dad ran right through a screen door, leaped three steps, and nearly broke his legs. I was too terrified to laugh at the situation. Dad limped for days and his face was scratched and swollen. Whatever he did to anger her, he never did it again!

There's a classic episode of the Andy Griffith Show where Opie kills a bird and he was so distraught when he could not make it fly again. He realized then that death is forever. I had a similar experience. One afternoon while exploring a wooded area near my home, I was looking for a target to shoot with my slingshot. Sometimes I would shoot old bottles or tin cans; paper or cardboard targets but a mockingbird's chirping caught my attention. Almost without thinking, I loaded my slingshot with a marble, aimed it and hit the bird. It fell to the ground; I picked it up and saw the damage that I had done. I realized it would never fly or sing again and I cried when I couldn't wish it back to life. I felt such great sorrow for what I had done that I buried the bird and threw away my

WINGS OF FAITH

slingshot. I never told anyone what I had done. As an adult, I now have five bird feeders in my yard and it brings me great joy to watch all the beautiful birds that come to my feeders. Every time I hear someone speak about the book or movie, To Kill a Mockingbird, I feel a pang of guilt.

Because they couldn't read or understand the Bible and were ashamed of their thrift store clothing, my parents did not go to church. They listened to preachers on the radio and sent me to Sunday school with the neighbor's children. I loved the Bible stories and fellowship with children who didn't call me ugly names. This was the first stepping stone in my spiritual journey. I loved going to church and I would go anytime I could. It did not matter to me which denomination. It brought me great comfort as I began learning to sing hymns and as I grew older I sang in my church choir for years.

My father became more and more reclusive. When people came to visit, Dad would hide in the bedroom until they left. It was so bad that he would not attend my high school graduation or my wedding. Dad was never comfortable around strangers. He was always afraid someone would ask him a question that he could not answer. He rarely had an opinion about anything. Like Greta Garbo, he just wanted to be "left alone."

Although we were poor, Mom would not accept charity from anyone. When people from the church I attended came by one day with a Thanksgiving basket with a turkey and all the trimmings, Mom would not accept it. She said there were people who needed it more than we did and so we had our usual pinto beans and boiled potatoes with skillet cornbread.

It is said that we are what we eat so I must be a mountain of beans! Mom always had a pot of beans soaking overnight

19

and my favorites were butter beans. I would eat them one at a time to savor the taste and make them last longer. I also liked boiled potatoes and I would often sneak one out of the pot for a night time snack. I drank a river of Kool-Aid as a child. It was cheap and it tasted good. My all time favorite food was Mom's custard pie. I have never tasted another one that can compare to those she made at Christmastime. Her recipes weren't written on paper, they were mostly in her head. Her other specialty during the holidays was skillet-fried peach pies with spices that made them irresistible.

One of my chores during the holidays was shelling bags of mixed nuts...pecans, walnuts, almonds, and the tough ones, Brazil nuts. I would spread out newspapers on the driveway or sidewalk and crack nuts for hours, picking out the precious nuts and putting them in jars. We would eat some and Mom would use some for baking.

WE MUST BE STRONG

We must believe when times are bad the best is yet to come
That side-by-side we march on with hearts beating like a drum.
We must be strong in times like these wherever we may trod
For faith is the tie that binds us in one nation under God.

WINGS OF FAITH

CHAPTER ONE

MAMA'S APRON STRINGS

(In memory: Laura Frances Harrison)
I followed Mama everywhere in my childhood days...
I learned to love and care from her unselfish ways.
I learned the joy of work, the peace of bedtime prayer...
From Mama's apron strings, I learned to give and share.
I learned respect for duty, the burdens one must bear...
I saw in her a beauty that on Earth is rare.
I learned one's word of honor is more valuable than gold...
The tender smiles she wore warmed me growing old.
I was my Mama's pride learning all those things...
Now she's gone, yet still I'm tied to Mama's apron strings!

The only person in my father's family that I ever met was Uncle Lee who lived in California but I did visit my mother's family in Tennessee twice on summer vacations. I loved seeing the countryside while looking out the window of a Greyhound Bus. It was wonderful to see new places and Tennessee was beautiful. After living in a big city, the country with its mountains and acres of fields and orchards was heavenly.

My grandfather, J. D. Vaughn, lived in a two story farm house at the foot of a mountain. The sunrises and sunsets were spectacular. Peaches were ripening in the orchard and the smell was divine. We had fresh vegetables from his garden with every meal. He grew tomatoes the size of softballs and we had fresh eggs from the hen house and milk fresh from the cows.

Hollyhocks grew wild in the fields and were taller than me. I saw my first hummingbird there and have loved them ever since. Rambling red roses grew beside split-rail fences as

21

WINGS OF FAITH

far as the eye could see and acres of Black Eyed Susan's ran beside the railroad tracks nearby. Before we returned to Tampa, my aunt Grace who lived in Na

shville, took me to the Grand Ole' Opry at the historic Ryman Auditorium. It was a three story brick building in the heart of town and the line to get in to the show stretched around the block. I saw many of Dad's favorite country singers in person but it would have been a dream come true if he had come with us. I wanted to stay in Tennessee forever but God had other plans for me.

THE SUMMER OF MY SIXTH YEAR

In the summer of my sixth year, I went to Tennessee
With Mom and Dad on a Greyhound bus, a special treat for me.
We were poor and times were bad so vacations were few.
Folks who had no education rarely had a dream come true.
For a city boy from Tampa, there was a lot to see
At Grandpa's farm near Nashville that changed the world for me.
There was a field of hollyhocks in colors bright and gay,
And everywhere were hummingbirds on aerial display.
I'd seen blue jays and mockingbirds and sea gulls by the bay,
But the fluorescent splendor of hummers blew me away!
The leap-frogging days of childhood are far behind me now,
But each time I see a hummingbird, I'm young again somehow.

WINGS OF FAITH

CHAPTER ONE

ON THE OUTSIDE LOOKING IN

Poverty can make or break you according to your will
For it takes determination to keep climbing uphill.
Waiting hours at a bus stop in the cold or summer rain,
Is a lesson in humility that rubs against the grain.
Upon the streets of circumstance, one struggles to survive
Living from payday to payday just to stay alive.
There are no frills when poverty rears its ugly head,
And dads must take a second job to keep their children fed.
Sometimes birthdays are forgotten and the cupboard is bare
When one lives from day to day on welfare and a prayer.
Poverty truly made me stronger knowing where I have been
For I survived my tender years on the outside looking in.

WINGS OF FAITH

CHAPTER 2

CALIFORINIA DREAMING

"I have fought a good fight, I have finished my race,
I have kept the faith." II Timothy 4:7 NIV

During my sixth grade summer break we were invited to spend two weeks with Uncle Lee in California, all expenses paid. It would become a vacation that lasted five years! We packed our suitcases, headed west, and rode the rails for three days and nights. Somewhere in California, approaching Los Angeles, I looked out the window and saw acres of California poppies blowing in  the wind. It looked like a scene from the Wizard of Oz and it took my breath away. I wondered then, with no houses anywhere in view, who had planted them.

Uncle Lee met us at the train station and took us to an apartment building he owned where we would spend our vacation. During the first week he somehow managed to talk Mom and Dad into staying in California. I was overjoyed but Mom didn't look too happy. We left nothing of value behind, but I saw a bright future ahead.

WINGS OF FAITH

That first week I learned a lot about my Uncle Lee. He was the oldest of seven children and he also hated life on the farm. As a young man with big dreams, he ran away from the farm and headed west, hitchhiking when funds were low. He landed a job as a studio driver in the early days of Hollywood where he drove actors wherever they needed to go. He invested his money in real estate, soon amassing a fortune. He bought an apartment building in Los Angeles, got his barber's license, and installed a barber shop on the ground floor.

Having studio contacts he was able to secure small acting jobs as an extra. By the 1950's, he owned stables in Beverly Hills, and a few rental properties in Los Angeles. He was skilled at dealing cards and blacksmithing which landed him small parts in many westerns. Years later he became an extra on Hill Street Blues where he posted some of my poems on the set's bulletin board. I wondered how a man like this could come from my father's family. He and my father were as different as night and day.

WINGS OF FAITH

Everything in California was completely different from Tampa. Uncle Lee located a two bedroom apartment for us to live in which was two blocks from the MGM Studios in Culver City. To my surprise, the schools were integrated! There were no "White's only" signs anywhere. How wonderful! Classes were harder but I maintained a B average, ran track, and made the cross country team. Not having a car gave me strong legs and stamina as I had to walk everywhere.

One of the major differences I discovered in Culver City was the affluence of the student body. The high school parking lot was filled with expensive cars. Students wore the "cool" clothes of the era. They were children who had wealthy, important parents, even movie stars like Ozzie and Harriet. Show business families were commonplace during Hollywood's "Golden Age." Ricky Nelson was on the tennis team in high school. His brother, David, was an acrobat. Almost every school in or near Los Angeles had notables in their student body.

The weather was an enigma. While days could be very hot, the temperature could drop forty degrees at night, and the humidity was low. Another curiosity was the smog. Sometimes the air seemed to be filled with tear gas. Still, it was better than the hot, humid summers I spent in Tampa sleeping on a couch on the porch in my underwear since we had no air conditioning.

Due to the diverse landscape in southern California, you could grow almost anything from figs and dates to citrus and grapes. Mom could now have an in ground, year round garden which gave her pleasure. Dad was a dishwasher by day and a night watchman at an aircraft factory. I suspected that Uncle Lee gave him an "allowance" on the side when money was short. I

26

still earned my spending money mowing the hilly lawns in the neighborhood.

I took chorus as an elective and loved the variety of music we sang from Stephen Foster to folk music and the early songs of rock 'n roll. I never had detention in school, but I did have one after school fight, which I lost. A football player who was a bully called me a "sissy" because I ran track rather than play football. He had no way of knowing I wanted to be a wide receiver but Mom wouldn't give consent to let me play. She thought it was too dangerous. She was probably right considering the news about brain damage these days. Gary, the bully, dared me to meet him after school behind the gym if I wasn't chicken. I knew I couldn't win, but I showed up anyway and a small crowd watched as I got pounded. No one ever called me "chicken" after that. My mother never knew it happened as my bruises were in places that didn't show.

I learned a life lesson in my freshman year from my cross country coach, Michael O'Rourke. Running 6.2 miles around the hillsides of Southern California is not for sissies. The training and conditioning were grueling. After wind sprints, stretching exercises, and laps around the vast school boundaries, we often took a school bus to a nearby beach to run in the sand and water. It was rather like the opening scene in Chariots of Fire. Cross country is a team sport as each team member scores points according to where he finishes in the pack and points are totaled when the race is over.

In my first competition, I was in third place at the halfway point ahead of all my teammates. I had visions of grandeur until I "hit the wall" about a mile from the finish line. I thought my lungs would explode! I could hardly breathe. Runners began passing me in bunches. I realized I had set too fast a pace and run out of gas. I slowed to a trot, a fast walk, and then I did the unforgivable and quit the race! Embarrassed, I sheepishly took a shortcut to our bus and contributed zero points to our team total. Coach O'Rourke found me; put an arm around my shoulder and explained that it's okay if you finish last, even if you walk or crawl across the finish line, but you NEVER QUIT! When you quit, you embarrass yourself, your team, and your school. "Learn to pace yourself and you'll be fine, he said." I never quit again. I worked extra hard and finished closer to the front of the pack with each race. I even held a few sprint records for a while.

[There is no failure except in not trying.]

NEVER QUIT!

Never quit when bad things happen; they happen every day
And there can be no victories for those who run away.
Never quit because you're frightened of things you can't control.
There's a higher Power within you to guide your heart and soul.
Never quit because the battle may be fought in pain.
David only had a slingshot when Goliath was slain!
Never quit because others doubt that you can win.
Keep the faith and you'll stand tall within the eyes of men,
Never quit because you're losing; the battle can be won
And it truly will amaze you what a little faith has done.
You will be an inspiration to others who may see
You didn't quit when things went wrong and won your victory!

A memorable family incident occurred shortly after we were living in Culver City. For some insane reason, my father came

28

WINGS OF FAITH

home one day in a car he had somehow borrowed. He could never get a driver's license, and I had no idea he even knew how to drive. Since Mom could read and therefore might be able to pass the driving test, he thought he could teach her to drive. He insisted she should get behind the wheel and he would talk her through it.

Most of California is not level ground. Our driveway had a steep, downward incline to the street. As soon as Mom was behind the wheel she froze. She took her foot off the brake and the car started rolling downhill, gaining speed. Dad was running alongside her screaming, "Step on the brake!" It was to no avail. Mom's hands froze on the steering wheel, keeping it straight, as the car rolled into the street, jumped the curb, crossed the neighbor's lawn, and came to rest in their living room! Since my mom didn't have a license or insurance, I do not know how no one went to jail; or who paid the damages to the neighbor's house and the borrowed car. I imagine Uncle Lee had a lot to do with it. From an outsider's point of view, the incident was quite hilarious but at the time, no one was laughing! Many women of Mom's generation never learned to drive. Shirley's mother and grandmother never drove a car. We have friends who refuse to drive, and that can be a real problem following the death of a spouse.

One afternoon some neighborhood boys asked if I would like to go with them to get autographs at MGM. It was 1953 and actors drove themselves to the studio and parked outside the main entrance across from the Irving Thalburg building. There were no throngs of paparazzi in those days, only a few neighborhood kids and an occasional tourist seeking autographs. I bought a ten cent autograph book and had the time of my life. My first autograph was from Elizabeth Taylor! She was the most beautiful woman I had ever seen and she

29

WINGS OF FAITH

was extremely nice. I would see her hundreds of times during the next five years.

That first day I also got autographs from Gene Kelly, Cyd Charisse, Van Johnson, Walter Pidgeon, Debbie Reynolds, and Marge and Gower Champion. I was on cloud nine...I was hooked. Almost every day after school and during summer breaks I met the MGM greats and visiting celebrities. One day, Humphrey Bogart pulled up in a sports car with a gigantic red bow on it for Lauren Bacall's birthday. She was filming Designing Woman at the time and she was thrilled with her new car, until it wouldn't start! So my friends and I pushed Bogie and Bacall down the street until the car started and watched them drive off into the sunset...what a memory!

My biggest thrill came one afternoon when I met John Wayne. It was getting dark as I started walking home. The Duke pulled up beside me and asked, "How far you going, kid?" I told him two blocks and he said, "Hop in, I'll take you home." When he pulled into my driveway, I asked if he would wait a minute so my mother could meet him. He said, "Sure, kid, I'd love to." He followed me into the house and my mom almost fainted!

In the spring of 1957 I met Rock Hudson at MGM. He had just returned from filming "Something of Value" in Africa. Beside him was a handsome young black man. As Rock Hudson signed my autograph book, he introduced me to the young man, Sidney Poitier. Rock Hudson was a box office superstar in the 1950's. He told me then that Sidney was destined to be a bigger star than he was in years to come because he was so talented. How right he was!

After James Dean completed filming his part in Giant, he attended a party at the studio. As he was walking back to his car,

30

WINGS OF FAITH

two teenage girls got into a fight. He threw down his cigarette and both of the girls attempted to retrieve it, destroying it in the process. A few weeks later, James Dean was killed in an automobile accident.

One afternoon, Elizabeth Taylor, who was married to producer Mike Todd, came out of the Thalberg building. Mr. Todd was carrying a cardboard box containing three adorable puppies. Miss Taylor knew me by name at that time and asked me if I would like to take one of the puppies home with me. Oh, how I would have loved to do that but I wasn't allowed to have pets in our rented home.

Katherine Hepburn would occasionally visit MGM while Spencer Tracy was filming there. Other than Greta Garbo, she was the most difficult autograph to acquire. She would refuse politely saying, "Sorry, I don't sign autographs." Now and then Spencer Tracy would tell her, "Come on Kate, give the kid a break." She would give him a harsh look and sign the autograph. I was one of the lucky ones to get one of those autographs, thanks to Mr. Tracy. I met Grace Kelly while she was filming her last movie, The Swan, in 1956. She was shy, almost bashful, but exuded the charisma that would define her the following year when she became Princess Grace of Monaco. Her natural beauty was undeniable. I was the only autograph seeker that evening as I walked with her to her car. I was truly fortunate to be at the right place at the right time. She had previously filmed High Society at the studio but I never caught a glimpse of her.

Outside the main gate at MGM, on a side street one block long, there was a bar that most people did not know existed. From time to time, studio security would need to go there and escort one of their stars back to the set. Gordon McRae and

WINGS OF FAITH

Lana Turner were "regulars." Making a movie is not always glamorous as they would spend an entire day filming only one scene. Seeing Hollywood stars in person on a daily basis for five years was exciting. I saw them with and without their makeup, and sometimes in full costume. MGM once boasted that they had more stars under contract than there were stars in the heavens. The studio was also known as "The Dream Factory." Among the married couples who were working there at the time I was getting autographs were Jean Simmons and Stewart Granger, Esther Williams and Fernando Lamas, Debbie Reynolds and Eddie Fisher, Cyd Charisse and Tony Martin, Elizabeth Taylor and Michael Wilding, and Marge and Gower Champion. Sadly, most of these marriages did not last. I realized at an early age that fame and fortune do not guarantee happiness.

Every autograph encounter with a celebrity becomes a memory. Now that "selfies" are in, memories go viral in a hurry. My five years of autograph collecting at MGM were wonderful. When I watch the great musicals filmed there, I remember having seen the actors in person the way they looked on the screen back then. Working security backstage at concert halls or having access to athletes on the field of play make for magical moments. I loved talking baseball with Ted Williams behind the batting cage while he managed the Washington Senators, or watching Roberto Clemente take batting practice. Getting baseballs signed was a real bonus later in life. I doubt that celebrities drive themselves to work or do their own grocery shopping anymore. Jerry Lewis used to play softball in a park near my home on weekends. Lloyd Bridges sat in the bleachers to watch Jeff and Beau play little league baseball. No one needed an entourage for protection...except Elvis at MGM when he filmed Jailhouse Rock.

WINGS OF FAITH

Those were wonderful years for me but Mom missed the South and wanted to return to Tampa. She never really made any friends in California; so once again, we packed suitcases for the trip back to Tampa. Our belongings, including my huge autograph collection, were crated up by a moving company and held in storage until we found a new home.

Several weeks later the truck arrived with everything, except my autograph collection. I was broken hearted. I had hundreds of one-of-a-kind movie stills from the great MGM musicals, all autographed. Although I had some of my favorite autograph books in my suitcase, what I lost would be priceless today. Through the years, I rebuilt my collection working security at venues, arenas, and sports stadiums. I have more than 50,000 autographs in my current collection, but nothing can replace the treasure trove that was lost in that move.

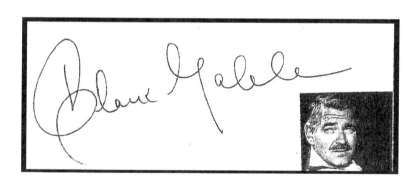

WINGS OF FAITH

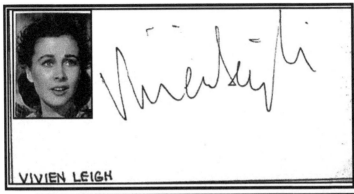

VIVIEN LEIGH

"STAGE DOOR"
LADY" "MAME"
"CRITIC'S
CHOICE"

"DUBARRY WAS A
"THE FACTS OF LIFE"
"YOURS, MINE AND OURS"
"FANCY PANTS"

LUCILLE BALL   "I LOVE LUCY" - TV SERIES

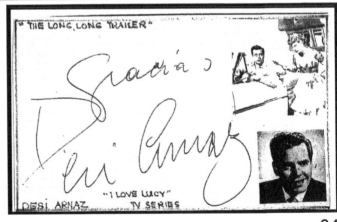

"THE LONG, LONG TRAILER"

DESI ARNAZ   "I LOVE LUCY"
TV SERIES

WINGS OF FAITH

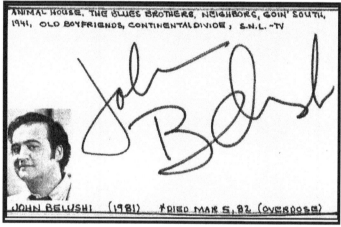

WINGS OF FAITH

WINGS OF FAITH

WINGS OF FAITH

WINGS OF FAITH

WINGS OF FAITH

WINGS OF FAITH

WINGS OF FAITH

WINGS OF FAITH

Don Williams
Marketing Art & Design
Walt Disney World
Post Office Box 40
Lake Buena Vista,
Florida 32830
November 10, 1985

Dear Clay,

I must apologize for taking so long to get back to you
on your request for Disney Characters. My schedule has
been hectic, but believe me, my intentions are good.
Enclosed -- a large size Bambi and an index size Jiminy
for your smaller album. I do hope that you will enjoy
them.

It was a pleasure to meet with you in Burdines, I only wish
that I would have had more time to chat with you and to take
a more thorough look through your albums. You have a fine
collection worth treasuring, something that I myself would
give my right arm for, as I also collect.

Again, please accept my apology for the delay, but as they
say, "better late than never."

Leaving Culver City was

Sincerely,

Don Williams
Don Williams

painful for me. After five

43

WINGS OF FAITH

years in one place, I felt at last I had established some roots. I made good friends for the first time in my life, I liked my school, and I loved having access to MGM Studios. I really liked Uncle Lee who took me to other studios and tourist attractions. I liked the warm days and cool nights. I didn't like the smog, especially when I was running cross country, but it came and went. Southern California was a nice place to live in the 1950's. It was as close to a Father Knows Best or Leave It to Beaver setting as one could find in the real world. The Korean War was far away and didn't dominate the evening news. On the home front, we felt safe watching I Love Lucy and variety shows that tickled our funny bones.

I visited every church within walking distance of my house and spent many hours on the playground of St. Augustine's Catholic Church across the street from my home. The nuns were very kind to me, even when my home runs broke a few convent windows. It was difficult to say goodbye to all my friends but God had other plans for me.

After hanging around MGM for five years I was confused about things I had seen and overheard. When actresses came for "auditions," they often returned to their cars in tears...both the ones who didn't get a coveted role in an upcoming movie and those who did get the part. I had heard the term, "casting couches" many times, but was too young and naïve to know what that meant. Powerful men ran the studios and actors did what they were told to do or they didn't work. Females earned much less than their male co-stars. Years later, as a police officer protecting celebrities at concerts, I was told how bad things were in the Golden Age of Hollywood. Today's "Me Too" movement has exposed those who abuse their power.

WINGS OF FAITH

MARILYN

Was it suicide or murder? Perhaps we'll never know
What happened on that fateful night so very long ago.
There are some who know her secret, but they will never tell
What happened in her bungalow the night the icon fell.
She was Alice in Wonderland who somehow lost her way
In the City of the Angels where stars can shine by day.
She was a dream girl for the ages with love affairs galore.
A president and a mobster slipped through her bedroom door.
From Norma Jean to Marilyn was a journey quite complex.
There were stumbling blocks and conflicts, and legendary sex.
What happened on that fateful night in nineteen sixty-two?
Was it suicide or murder? We still don't have a clue!

WINGS OF FAITH

CHAPTER 3

THE BIRTH OF A POET

*"Commit thy works unto the Lord,
and thy thoughts shall be established."*
Proverbs 16:3 NIV

Cukver City Junior High School

I must confess I was a bit depressed moving back to Tampa where I enrolled in Thomas Jefferson High School following the Christmas break in 1957. Settling into a new school is always stressful. Coming from an integrated school in California to a segregated school with a large Latino student body made me an outsider once again.

WINGS OF FAITH

I made the track team and was part of the four member 440 relay team. In the decade to come, all four of us would be officers of the Tampa Police Department. In Culver City, we had a stadium with a first class cinder track and a huge campus surrounded by olive trees. At Jefferson, we had a gym for basketball games but no track. We had to jog to a dirt field four blocks from the school to train for our track meets. The coaches called me "California" that first year. They were debating the merits of establishing a wrestling team, and during physical education classes, we were paired off in the gym to see who had potential as a wrestler. At 140 pounds, I was built for speed, not wrestling, and I was paired against the largest kid in school who was an amateur boxer. He bullied kids in his classes. I felt like David getting ready to face Goliath. Overcome by fear, my adrenaline kicked in and I managed to get Gonzo in a headlock and held on for dear life. He tried to break the hold but I squeezed with all my strength. It had to be divine intervention because he was about to pass out when the coach stopped the match. I was afraid of after school repercussions but to my surprise, he shook my hand and said, "You're all right, California." I had gained his respect and the respect of my classmates, but I kept looking over my shoulder walking home from school that day.

The curriculum at Jefferson in 1957 was so much easier than it was in California. As a result, I was always on the honor roll, and things I studied in junior high school were being taught in high school in Tampa. Jefferson had the best marching band in the state of Florida at that time and the best baseball team in the county. Many major leaguers came from the Tampa Bay area. Tony La Russa was Jefferson's best player who became one of the great baseball managers of all time.

WINGS OF FAITH

It was the era of rock 'n roll and Jefferson had two bands that played for many sock hops in the area and beyond. There was a sandwich shop located a block from the school where students gathered before classes. We would play the juke box, dance, and enjoy a cup of Cuban coffee with a guava turnover. At lunchtime, some students left the three story red brick school building to grab a Cuban sandwich. Since I worked in the school cafeteria I got free lunches. I stayed after school during track and field season to train for the track meets. Tampa had no cross country teams. Running 6.2 miles on flat ground would have been a walk in the park after running around those California mountains. I wrote a term paper about long distance running called "Grueling Grandeur," which detailed the history of the Olympic Games.

I believe God made me fast for a purpose. I was walking home from a weekly Bible study at a friend's house one evening and cut through a neighborhood park. A grubby, homeless man came out of the shrubs, pulled out a switchblade and asked me for my wallet. I didn't even have a wallet so I just took off running and left him in the dust. I ran all the way home! The next week I took a different route to my Bible study. We had a Bible Club at Jefferson that met after school once a week. Many of us met for morning prayers by the flag pole before classes began. I also joined the Junior Lions Club and Shirley and I were members of the Lions Club many years later.

I had always been a loner, had little money, and girls were not attracted to me. In my junior year, I played basketball after school at a neighborhood playground. I began noticing a pretty blonde sitting on a bench watching our games. I felt like she was watching me more than the game and I found it difficult to focus. When I walked home, she walked the same direction.

WINGS OF FAITH

I discovered she had moved into a house one block from mine. But, because she lived on the opposite side of the street, she was in a different school district and went to Plant High School which was a Jefferson rival.

I began spending more time with Pauline and less time playing basketball. Soon we were "going steady." We played records at her house after school and went to movies on weekends. She hid a blue plastic box in a shrub in front of her house each morning. On school days, we left notes for each other. When I passed by, I took out her note and replaced it with mine.

Before the end of the school year I found out how much a teenage romance can hurt. I came home from school one day and found Pauline and her father waiting in my living room. I knew something was wrong when I saw the tears in her eyes. Her father, a photographer, had received a good job offer and they were moving right away...to New Orleans. It might as well have been to the moon! We were forbidden to contact each other and were told it would only prolong our pain.

There were no cell phones or computers in those days. It was hopeless. I knew Pauline would try to write me but my mother always got the mail and would destroy her letters. I came home from school one day and realized Mom had taken Pauline's pictures from my room and destroyed them. That really hurt. I spent many sleepless nights wondering what might have been. It was a short lived romance, but one I'll never forget. Pauline reminded me of a young Betty Hutton who starred in the Perils of Pauline and the Greatest Show on Earth.

WINGS OF FAITH

CHAPTER THREE

In my senior year, I learned that God had plans for me and my spiritual journey would soon hit fast forward. I got to "ham it up" in the opera, Il Trovatore. The Sun State Opera Federation, based in Tampa, brought Salvatore Baccaloni to town to star in the production. Local church male choir members were recruited to fill in the supporting cast. At that time, I was singing in the Jefferson High School chorus and also the choir at my church. I was chosen for a small part and enjoyed the experience immensely, even the heavy stage makeup and costuming as well as a lesson in sword fighting. It was a treat seeing my name (in small print) on the program with a renowned opera star like Baccaloni. I also sang in a high school production of Oklahoma and in the community choir at the Billy Graham Crusade which changed my life later that year.

While singing in my church choir, I was truly blessed to sit beside Wilbur Denning, otherwise known as the Singing Mailman. In those days, the mail carriers delivered mail on foot in residential neighborhoods thus causing many friendships to develop. While walking his route, Wilbur sang hymns and became quite the celebrity. He had a beautiful voice and I

was delighted to sit next to him in our choir loft. Every Easter he sang his signature hymn, "The Holy City" with so much emotion that it brought tears to many eyes. Whenever I hear that hymn, I can close my eyes and imagine Wilbur giving it his all.

There were several venues that featured teen idols like Fabian, Lou Christie, Dion and the Belmonts,

WINGS OF FAITH

etc. Dick Clark also brought a group of Bandstand idols to town each year in the late 1950's. It was the era of 45 records and long playing vinyl albums with designer record jackets. Many of these still reside in my home tucked away in a closet.

The National Guard Armory had several shows each year featuring country singers like Jim Reeves, Marty Robbins, Johnny Cash, etc. These were the only shows my father would attend. I never heard my parents sing along with anyone on the radio or pray out loud. I have no memory of either of them ever saying "I love you" to me or to each other. Love was expressed by actions rather than words.

My advanced English teacher, Ethel Schilling, was a take-no-prisoners disciplinarian. She tolerated no foolishness in her classroom and when she walked down the halls of Jefferson High, it was like the parting of the Red Sea. Students got out of her way. She praised no one's work and rarely gave anyone an A. She was there to teach, not to "coddle."

One day we were studying poetry and Mrs. Schilling was reading "Little Boy Blue" by Eugene Field, a poem about the death of a child. By the time she got to the second verse, tears were flowing from her eyes and running down her cheeks. You could have heard a pin drop in the room. The silence was deafening. It was an epiphany for me to realize how much power a poem could have on someone, even the stern and rigid Mrs Schilling. I had no idea how much that moment would impact my life in the near future.

WINGS OF FAITH

CHAPTER THREE

MRS. SCHILLING

She was five-foot-two of attitude with dark, soul-piercing eyes,
A Bette Davis look-alike who'd take no alibis.
She ruled her classroom like a tsar when teens thought they were "cool"
While Ike was in the White House and prayer was still in school.
Students who took her English class worked hard to earn an A
She taught both prose and poetry from Steinbeck to Millay.
Her countenance was icy cold; we never saw her smile.
We never heard her tell a joke for that was not her style.
One day she read "Little Boy Blue" and took us by surprise,
For on verse two she bowed her head as tears flowed from her eyes!
We sat there in stunned silence, some staring at the wall.
We'd seen a metamorphosis-she was human after all!

GOOD TEACHERS

Good teachers teach life lessons not found in any book.
They help us find simple truths that others overlook.
They help us see the "big picture" one piece at a time,
And prepare us for the mountains we may have to climb.

During that school year, my mother took in washing and ironing and babysat our neighbor's two year old daughter, Lorraine Garcia, whom I adored. For me, she was the little sister I never had. When she was diagnosed with a liver disease, I was devastated. She passed away before her third birthday.

52

WINGS OF FAITH

I remembered the poem Mrs. Schilling had read and was inspired to write my first poem, "Little Lorraine."

The Garcia family owned a printing company and liked my poem so much they printed it on a fancy card and passed it out at Lorraine's funeral service. I showed it to Mrs. Schilling and she assured me that I definitely had a talent for writing poetry. She encouraged me to submit poems to the school newspaper. I was on my way to becoming a poet.

LITTLE LORRAINE

Little Lorraine had eyes of blue that sparkled like morning dew
And every time she smiled at me, it was a lovely sight to see.
Little Lorraine was only two the night she passed away.
Never again will those eyes of blue sparkle and look my way.
She has gone to meet her Maker somewhere beyond the blue.
She has gone to treasures greater since her work on earth is through.
She was an angel in disguise who came but could not stay
For I saw heaven in her eyes before she passed away!

The following poem is the first one I wrote for the Jefferson High newspaper.

53

GOD'S GIFT

An everlasting gift was given,
　Of a Savior who has long since risen.

His birthday will soon be celebrated,
　But its true meaning isn't always stated.

Some people think Christmas is such a bore;
　They give presents, but nothing more.

They sometimes fail to realize
　That the world wasn't worthy of its sacred prize.

The world in chaos and turmoil had been,
　Ruled by men who thrived on sin.

The Child whose crib was a manger
　Was to millions a perfect stranger.

But following a Star came Three So Wise
　To worship the Child with happy cries.

This Child born in a mound of hay
　Gave the world its first Christmas Day.

He gave His life on Calvery
　So that we could live eternally!

We celebrate His birthday still;
　And I pray that we always will.

May the Christ in Christmas be clear and plain
　To tell the world He didn't die in vain!

By Clay Harrison

WINGS OF FAITH

CHAPTER THREE

During the Lenten season that year, our youth group from Tampa Heights United Methodist Church attended the world famous Black Hills Passion Play at the Lake Wales amphitheater. I couldn't afford a ticket but my pastor, Eugene Rutland, paid my way saying, "You need to see this play." This would soon become a divine intervention.

As the crucifixion scene unfolded and Christ was on the cross, a thunderstorm suddenly appeared. Chaos reigned as people ran for cover. After the intermission, the storm vanished as quickly as it had appeared. When the play resumed and Christ was being taken off the cross, the most brilliant rainbow I've ever seen appeared over the amphitheater! It was mind blowing! Even the actors paused to look at it. I had goose bumps galore! The Holy Spirit was tugging at my heartstrings and I was primed for what would happen next.

Josef Meier
WORLD FAMOUS
CHRISTUS PORTRAYER

BLACK HILLS PASSION PLAY • P.O. Box 489 • Spearfish, South Dakota 57783 • Phone 605/642-3646

August 16, 1991

Dear Mr. Harrison:

I apologize for the delay in sending a picture to you but your name and address had been misplaced and just recently was located again. Trusting all is well with you, I remain,

Yours in Christ,

Guido Della Vecchia

Guido Della Vecchia

WINGS OF FAITH

Later that month a Billy Graham crusade had been scheduled at Philip's Field (a racetrack which no longer exists) by the Hillsborough River. I was in the choir that night. Ethel Waters sang, "His Eye Is on the Sparrow," and later George Beverly Shea sang, "Victory in Jesus." The goose bumps were back! Like John Wesley, my heart too was "strangely warmed!" I want "Victory in Jesus" sung at my memorial service when my spiritual journey has ended.

Even before Dr. Graham rose to deliver his sermon, I was ready to accept Jesus Christ as my Lord and Savior! Pastor Rutland baptized me a few weeks later. There are no coincidences when God reveals His plan for your life. You truly are a "new creation" born of the Spirit.

As I am writing this CHAPTER in February 2018, The Rev. Billy Graham passed away at the age of 99. He will be greatly missed. Unlike many evangelists, Dr. Graham never allowed himself to become the subject of a scandal. He wasn't in it for the money or the women. He was never alone in a room with a woman other than his wife Ruth. Many years later when he came to Tampa for a crusade at Tampa Stadium, I was on his security detail and saw this first hand.

Shortly after my baptism, I discovered the sermons of Peter Marshall, the former pastor of New York Avenue Presbyterian Church in Washington D.C. He was also the chaplain of the United States Senate in the late 1940's. When I saw the movie, "A Man Called Peter," the story of his life and tragic death, I began to read every book I could find about him including his sermons and prayers, and everything his wife, Catherine, wrote until her death.

Dr. Marshall's sermons, Mr. Jones, Meets the Master, By Invitation of Jesus, and Keepers of the Springs, about the value of godly women, impacted me greatly as a teenager sprouting my wings of faith.

In the late 1950's churches held more revivals than they do now. Well known evangelists like Ford Philpot and Bob Harrington would hold week long services with lots of hymn singing. A feature of the Methodist church that I miss the most is coming up to the altar for prayer time during the Sunday evening services. These days, many churches do not have an altar which is sad because there is something very special about praying at an altar.

I found peace and joy at an early age even though there would be hardships and mountains yet to climb. But now I had blessed assurance that I would not have to climb them alone. When graduation day arrived in 1960, it was a proud day for me as I was graduating with honors. I took my cap and gown and rode a bus, alone, to receive my diploma at the National Guard Armory. Mom and Dad stayed home. There was no celebration.

Dad had been "feeling poorly" and he found it difficult to keep up with his duties as a dishwasher and janitor at the Gator Bar and Restaurant which closed at 2 a.m. It was located on the waterfront in a dangerous part of town. During the last few weeks of school, in the evenings after finishing my homework, I walked to the Gator Bar to help Dad.

At closing time, I put up the chairs and stools, swept and mopped, while he finished washing the dishes and cleaning the restrooms. Then we would walk home together around

57

WINGS OF FAITH

three in the morning. Police officers in their patrol cars would often stop us and ask why we were walking in such a dangerous area at that time of the morning. I couldn't resist replying, "We're walking because we don't have a car!" For some reason, they failed to see the humor in that. A short time later, Dad got a job washing dishes at Mave's Five & Ten in Sulphur Springs. It was a daytime job and he could ride a bus to work. In later years, my wife and I would buy our children's stocking stuffers at Mave's.

Dad was a man of few words but he enjoyed working in kitchens, keeping things clean, and took pride in making things shine. He took "cleanliness is next to Godliness" seriously.

[Every disappointment offers a lesson.]

THERE IS DIGNITY IN LABOR

There is dignity in labor as there is in management.
There's honor in a hard days work because it pays the rent.
Someone has to clean the bathrooms and take the trash away.
Someone has to wash the dishes and stock the shelves each day.
Someone has to dig the ditches and sweep and mop the floor.
Someone has to check you out each time you leave the store.
We can't all be management and wear a three-piece suit.
Without the migrant workers, who would pick the fruit?
For everyone in the spotlight, there are many we don't see
Who are never recognized for their work and loyalty.
While some seek fame and fortune, most work to pay the rent...
There is dignity in labor as there is in management.

WINGS OF FAITH

CHAPTER THREE

POETIC JUSTICE

My car is old and weary, showing signs of wear and tear,
But though it's sad and dreary, it somehow gets me there.
Others ride in luxury content to beep and pass,
And oh, how it tickles me to pass them out of gas!

"Commit thy works unto the Lord, and thy thoughts shall be
established." Prov. 16:3 NIV
I try my best to live by this Proverb.

After graduation, I worked at Bentley-Grey Wholesale Dry Goods until they downsized. Since I was the last salesman hired, I was the first one to be laid off. My next job was at a Grand-Way store where I did everything from unloading trucks to stocking shelves, and bagging groceries.

College was out of the question as I wasn't a star athlete and I didn't want to incur a student loan. Looking back, I realize it was all part of God's plan. How was I to know that when we were moving back to Tampa from California, the girl I would one day marry was moving to Tampa from West Virginia.

Sometimes an ordinary day can become extraordinary in a heartbeat. It happened one day at Grand-Way when I literally ran into my wife to be and immediately apologized for knocking her down. There was chemistry between us, an instant connection. Our eyes met and something electric passed between us. Shirley was only thirteen at the time while I was nineteen but she was mature for her age. However, she went her way and I went back to work.

WINGS OF FAITH

In the following weeks, I saw her in the store more and more often and we talked a little when I had time. Later on as when we began dating, her mom liked me right away but her dad wasn't so easily won over. Fathers of thirteen year old girls are rightfully cautious. The irony was that he started dating Shirley's mom at that same age. They eloped and married while she was still in high school and kept their marriage secret for a year. He was six years older than her with ten days between their birthdays. So it was with Shirley and me. It became a family tradition.

Since Shirley lived within walking distance of Grand-Way, I would often walk to her house after work, have dinner with them and take a later bus home. Her dad would drive us to ball games at her school, to the beach, or to a movie on weekends. When she turned fifteen, we were allowed to "go steady." By the time she was sixteen, I began to stay later in the evenings often sitting on the front porch swing with her dad peeking out the window. I had to walk over a mile to catch the last bus home and since I was often late leaving, I would miss the last bus, and have to walk three more miles. I always considered that extra goodnight kiss worth it! I wrote many poems for Shirley throughout the years and she still has them.

In 1963, President Kennedy started a physical fitness program for America. People were walking and biking across the country. The city of Tampa held a 50 mile fitness walk across Tampa Bay to Clearwater and back, sponsored by a local radio station. I volunteered to represent Grand-Way in the walk and carried a poster-sized sign that read, "Go Grand-Way, all the way!"

Thousands lined up at dawn for the walk. There were check points every five miles where they placed a check mark by

WINGS OF FAITH

your name. At the half way point in Clearwater, buses were provided to bring people back who weren't able to continue and hundreds dropped out.

On the return to Tampa, I gained on, and passed, many people. I thought I was the winner only to find out that two college boys had finished a half hour earlier, claimed the prize money, and disappeared. It was determined later that they were driven the last five miles by a roommate and missed the last checkpoint.

Grand-Way published a nice story about me in their national Grand Union magazine, and I received a personal letter from the company president, Thomas Butler, who thanked me for the poem I wrote about the experience.

Growing up without a family car and my training for the cross country team in California helped prepare me for this moment. Coach O'Rourke's voice reminding me to "never quit" would echo through my ears during the second half of the walk when the miles seemed to multiply.

I was on duty at Grand-Way the day President Kennedy was assassinated. It was a day of mourning nationwide. After work, I was invited to ride with other employees to pray at Sacred Heart Catholic Church in downtown Tampa. The church was aglow with candlelight and filled with mourners with tear dimmed eyes. Americans were united like never before.

The President had visited Tampa a short time before going to Dallas. He broke away from his Secret Service detail to shake hands with the crowds and signed a few autographs. His tragic death was one of the most memorable days in history since Pearl Harbor, and a precursor to Nine-Eleven,

WINGS OF FAITH

three days that will live in infamy. The image of "John-John" saluting his father's casket passing by will forever be etched in the hearts of all who witnessed it.

"John-John" salutes the passing casket on November 25, his third birthday,

WINGS OF FAITH

CHAPTER THREE

WE WEPT EACH OTHER'S TEARS
(Nov. 22, 1963)

We wept each other's tears the day they killed J.F.K.
We were a nation in mourning for our president that day.
We came together in our sorrow because once upon a time
There was a D.C. Camelot with happy days sublime.
They were the perfect family with a future bright and gay
Until that Dallas motorcade one fateful autumn day.
Shots rang out and chaos reigned; we would never be the same.
We wept each other's tears that day and wondered who to blame.
Who can say what was lost that day – there was no turning back.
A bright and rosy future had faded into black.
For one brief and shining moment in our storied history,
We caught a glimpse of Camelot and American royalty.

WINGS OF FAITH

CHAPTER 4

FOR GOD AND COUNTRY

*"Greater love hath no man than this,
that a man lay down his life for his friends." John 15:13 NIV*

534th MP Company, Ft. Clayton

Basic Training: Fort Jackson, S.C.

America was embroiled in the Vietnam War in 1963. It was an era of political unrest, civil rights marches and assassinations. Draft dodgers were making hasty retreats to Canada, or family doctors were creating fake injuries to keep rich kids out of the draft. I was 1-A, healthy, and not in college, so I took a three year enlistment in the United States Army. It was the right thing to do for God and Country. Shirley cried, my mother cried, and I choked back tears when I left for Ft. Jackson, South Carolina.

Basic training is a humbling experience. I was in Company C, also known as Maddox's Raiders. Sgt. Maddox was determined that we would outshine Company A and B. We got up earlier, did our Army daily dozen exercises before breakfast, and marched five miles to the rifle range in full gear while the other companies rode in Army trucks.

Everyone did their turn at KP duty scrubbing pots and pans big enough to stand in. By the time you got them clean, the cooks messed them up again for the next meal. You were exhausted by the evening.

Getting used to Army boots was painful. I developed an ingrown toenail; the doctor cut it out with no pain killer, put a huge band aid on it, and sent me out to our daily close-order drills with a bloody sock. The infiltration course was difficult at that time, crawling under barbed wire with explosions all around and machine gun fire overhead. We were restricted to the base during basic training but we were too tired to go anywhere anyway.

Ft. Gordon

WINGS OF FAITH

CHAPTER FOUR

I came home for two weeks leave after Basic then returned to Ft. Gordon for eight weeks of Military Police training. Again tears were shed, and as usual, my father stayed home.

Soldiers were not considered heroes in those days. The Masters was underway when I arrived for military police training in Augusta which GI's called "Disgusta." There was a sign in the park entrance outside the base stating in bold letters, "NO DOGS OR GI'S ALLOWED."

THEY DIDN'T CALL US HEROES

They didn't call us heroes in the war with Vietnam,
But the killing fields and booby traps were no night at the prom.
We didn't burn our draft cards or leave the U.S.A.;
We took an oath to do or die and ventured in harm's way.
They didn't call us heroes while we were over there.
They burned our flag in effigy and cursed us everywhere.
We sacrificed our futures to answer duty's call.
We shed our blood and sweat and tears and watched our brothers fall.
We lived through hell and paid our dues for freedom is not free,
But they didn't call us heroes in nineteen sixty-three!

We had our daily exercises but we were treated better at MP school. The focus was on military law and Army history. The food was also better and we didn't have to pull KP duty. Our graduating class was scheduled to go to Germany but when riots broke out in Panama, we were dispatched to reinforce our troops there. We took a train to Brooklyn where we boarded a Navy ship and the MP's were assigned to guard duty. Walking the decks at night was awe inspiring to me as I saw stars and constellations I had never seen on land before. Unlike the

WINGS OF FAITH

Army, the Navy served midnight chow which I really enjoyed.

I was stationed at Ft. Clayton across the highway from the Miraflores Locks in Panama. From my window on the third floor of the barracks, I could watch ocean liners pass through the locks. The 534th MP Company patrolled bases on the Pacific side of the zone and patrolled inside the Republic with the Guardia Nacional keeping GI's out of "off limits" establishments. During my tour of duty in Panama, I won six Soldier of the Month awards from Company to Command level.

WINGS OF FAITH

DEPARTMENT OF THE ARMY
HEADQUARTERS UNITED STATES ARMY FORCES SOUTHERN COMMAND
OFFICE OF THE COMMANDER
FORT AMADOR, CANAL ZONE

IN REPLY REFER TO

SCARGA

SUBJECT: Letter of Recognition

TO: Specialist Fourth Class Clayton Harrison
RA 14867355
534th Military Police Co (Svc)
Fort Clayton, Canal Zone

1. As your Commander, I am pleased to note that, from all the fine troops assigned to this Command, you have been selected as "United States Army Forces Southern Command Soldier of the Month".

2. As you well know, the selection process is a detailed one, commencing with your own unit and culminating in the final selection by the NCO Council of the Command. That you emerged from this processing as the outstanding soldier in USARSO speaks highly of your training, your interest and your soldierly qualities. You have set an example not only for the men of your own group, but for all personnel of the Command. In these perilous times in our Nation's history, it is obvious that the men of our Armed Forces must be of the highest caliber. That you demonstrated these qualities is evidenced by your selection as the Soldier of the Month, I compliment you.

3. As you know, recognition of your selection takes the form of a United States Savings Bond, this letter of congratulations from me, and your appointment as my Enlisted Aide for a week. In the latter capacity, you will accompany me on an official visit to one of the Latin American countries at a later date.

4. Again, you have my congratulations and my best wishes for continued success during your service to our Country in our Army.

J. D. ALGER
Major General, USA
Commanding

Sometimes it was disturbing to read American newspapers and see what was happening back in the states. Young men were training to fight, and maybe die, in Vietnam. The "hippies" were burning draft cards, women were burning their bras, and everyone was burning the American flag.

The 1960's brought the "summer of love" with peace marches, sit-ins, and protest songs. Jane Fonda made headlines sitting on a tank and became known as "Hanoi Jane." I know a pastor who still thinks of her in that way. I would meet her many years later when she came to Tampa for the Super Bowl and she confessed that she would never be able to live down that incident.

WINGS OF FAITH

CHAPTER FOUR

WHAT DID THEY DIE FOR IN VIETNAM?

What did they die for in Vietnam? Was it worth the sacrifice?
Where was the honor and glory that came at such a price?
"There's no such thing as Agent Orange!" the politicians said,
But looking back across the years how many more are dead?
They didn't burn their draft cards or our flag in effigy.
When duty called, they went to war and sailed across the sea.
And now their names are on the wall in Washington, D.C.!
They paid the price, but for what? Who did their dying free?
Nobody called them heroes when they came limping home.
There were no crowds to cheer them beneath some fancy dome.
How many lives were shattered then; have we gone and done it twice?
What did they die for in Vietnam; was it worth the sacrifice?

VOICES FROM THE WALL

How frequently you come here now and stand in reverie
Remembering the love we shared in nineteen sixty-three.
Sometimes I watch you trace my name engraved here on the wall.
You leave behind a tear stained rose each time you leave the Mall.
I know you often ask yourself how different things would be
If there had been no war in 'Nam in nineteen sixty-three.
We'll never know what might have been, nor can we change the past,
For some must die that others live once the die is cast.
You cannot live in the past remembering the dead
For the future's bright before you and you must forge ahead.
Be happy now with your new love for it was meant to be
When I became a memory in nineteen sixty-three.

WINGS OF FAITH

11 September 1973

Dear Mr. Harrison:

Mrs. Bradley and I are deeply grateful for your concern and good wishes during my illness.

Thank you for your thoughtfulness.

Sincerely,

Omar N Bradley

OMAR N. BRADLEY
General of the Army

Long periods of separation contribute to marital infidelity. That and post traumatic stress lead to a great number of military suicides unless one was well grounded in their faith. I worked one tragic case where a Marine got a "Dear John" letter. His wife was pregnant by another man while he was on active duty at Ft. Amador. He got very drunk, laid down on the railroad tracks in front of an approaching train. It was a gory scene. It's said that "absence makes the heart grow fonder," but not in that case.

WINGS OF FAITH

CHAIRMAN OF THE JOINT CHIEFS OF STAFF

WASHINGTON, D. C. 20318-9999

3 September 1993

Dear Mr. Harrison,

Thank you for the kind letter of support. It is always nice to hear from our veterans. Please accept my personal thanks for your continuing service to our Nation as a police officer.

I have autographed your card, and am enclosing a photograph and returning your stamped envelope. I appreciate your taking the time to write.

With best wishes,

Sincerely,

COLIN L. POWELL
Chairman
of the
Joint Chiefs of Staff

WINGS OF FAITH

My best friend was Walter Jones, our unofficial barrack's chaplain. He was the calming voice of reason when tempers flared and someone was out of line. Walter prayed for those who went to town to "sow their wild oats." When I began to acquire a taste for rum and coke at the NCO Club, he reminded me that Christians need to "walk the walk" in order to "talk the talk."I began attending the Christian Servicemen's Home in the Zone and never drank alcohol again.

There were no smart phones or laptops during that era so information was slow getting to military posts. American music was changing greatly in the age of "sex, drugs, and rock 'n roll" and "make love, not war." GI's were listening to artists like Cat Stevens, Richie Havens, Joan Baez, Judy Collins, and Barry McGuire's "The Eve of Destruction" which could describe today's politics and world affairs.

I had the pleasure of escorting Green Beret Staff Sergeant Barry Sadler around Ft. Clayton after his "Ballad of the Green Berets" became a big hit. I still find myself humming that song once in a while. The Green Berets also trained for Vietnam in Panama because the jungles were so similar. Panama also had some areas that were off limits to everyone as a tribe of headhunters lived there. I saw monkeys, anteaters, iguanas, boas, and a sloth while I was there. In the evenings, legions of bats took flight and when the rainy season began, the roads were littered with thousands of beetles and frogs.

From time to time PBS will broadcast music from this era and I'm transported back to that time. A jungle can be very beautiful but it can also be deadly at the same time. Nights seem to have a music all their own. Birds and other animals communicate with one another in various ways. In war time, the next sound you hear could be your last.

WINGS OF FAITH

CHAPTER FOUR

When I came home on leave at the end of my tour of duty in Panama, I proposed to Shirley, who was now nineteen. We started counting down the days until I was a civilian once more. My friend, Walter, returned home and became a minister.

I spent the last eight months of my Army career at Ft. Sam Houston in San Antonio, Texas. Within the quadrangle at the entrance to the base, there is a tower where Geronimo was once imprisoned. Deer and peacocks freely roamed the quadrangle while I was stationed there.
I experienced my first (and only) sandstorm there, and nearly froze when temperatures dropped to six degrees before we were authorized to wear our winter uniforms.

Texans were more tolerant of soldiers. I was treated far better than when I was in Georgia. We could actually leave the base without being cursed or spat on, but we wore civilian clothes when we were off duty.

Downtown San Antonio was interesting and the River Walk was delightful. The Alamo was a disappointment as the city was completely built up around the mission, making it difficult to visualize the battle that had been waged there.

My military police duties were mostly routine. I did get to pick up AWOL's in Houston and Ft. Hood and transport them back to San Antonio, but I had no life threatening situations while stationed there.

I received my corporal stripes at Ft. Sam which made me an NCO, and I was promised sergeant stripes if I re-upped before my tour of duty came to an end. They could have offered

WINGS OF FAITH

to make me a general and I would have said, "No, thanks" because I was getting married to Shirley and I could hardly wait.

Mail call was my favorite time of the day. Shirley's letters came with W.A.T. written on the back flap which stood for "We're Almost There" based on a song by Andy Williams. I was discharged from the Army on St. Patrick's Day and we were married on March 31st. Shirley was a beautiful bride and I considered myself the luckiest man on earth! Coming home on St. Patrick's Day brings special memories to me.

WINGS OF FAITH

CHAPTER 5

LOVE AND MARRIAGE

*Therefore shall a man leave his father and mother,
and shall cleave unto his wife and they shall be one flesh."
Genesis 2:24 NIV*

When I came home from the service, I was in for quite a shock. There was a stranger in my house! Without telling me, my parents had divorced and both had remarried; my Mother on Valentine's Day, just six weeks before I came home. Shirley was sworn to secrecy and was loyal to her future mother-in-law.

Unfortunately, Mom married a con man. It was obvious to me, but love is blind and she couldn't see it. Neal wouldn't work

WINGS OF FAITH

and he had squandered the monthly allotments I sent home during my tour of duty. He was also a compulsive liar; he lied about everything for no apparent reason. As a result, we spent less time at their house.

My father married a woman he met in Sulphur Springs at the Mave's department store who had spent most of her life in mental institutions. Neither was a marriage made in heaven.

Shirley and I were married on March 31, 1967, at North Rome Baptist Church in Tampa. It was a marriage made in heaven! She was a beautiful bride, the answer to my prayers. I now had someone to share my faith journey. More than fifty years have passed since that day and I love her more than ever! We hold hands wherever we go. Now and then someone will approach us on the street and say what a cute couple we make.

We had neither time nor money for a honeymoon. It would be postponed for thirty-four years until we had our first tour of Europe. It was worth the wait. Our first home was a garage apartment on Central Avenue. It was across from Hillsborough High School where I proposed to Shirley. That was her high school. She was brave enough to wear my Jefferson High School letterman's sweater to classes there. We had few belongings in our garage apartment but we didn't need much that early in our marriage.

"Therefore shall a man leave his mother and father, and shall cleave unto his wife and they shall be one flesh." Genesis 2:24 NIV

WINGS OF FAITH

Shirley's grandparents,
Frank and Myrtle Lanham

Shirley with her mother,
Drema Huddleston

Shirley with her father,
Wilson Huddleston

When I entered the Tampa Police Academy, Shirley took a secretarial job at the Chamber of Commerce. She got free tickets to Florida attractions which were a real plus since police officers didn't earn much money in those days. Upon graduation from the Academy, I was chosen class speaker and spoke about John 15:13..."Greater love hath no man than this, that a man lay down his life for others." We knew any one of us could one day make the supreme sacrifice in order to "serve and protect."

To me, law enforcement was a ministry...serve and protect the innocent; apprehend and prosecute the guilty. I carried copies of my Salesian Inspirational books and gave them to crime victims. I even wrote poems inspired by them. Without faith and a loving wife, I doubt I could have survived 32 years as a police officer in Tampa. Seeing "man's inhumanity to man" sometimes broke my heart, but bringing comfort to crime victims and seeing justice done brought me joy.

My faith journey took me down some mean streets and dark alleys. To say I was never afraid would be a lie, but by faith, I always had courage to perform under fire while in harm's way. We had no "bullet proof" vests in those days, and even had to buy our own equipment.

THE KEY

The key was in the mailbox
Now a killer's in the den,
A body's in the bedroom
Where the key should have been.

My six months probationary period was spent walking the beat on Franklin Street where I once lived as a toddler. Thankfully it wasn't as wild as it had been back then. Call boxes had been replaced with hand held radios and officers were better trained in self defense.

In 1969, I partnered with a street-smart officer, Romeo Cole, Jr. His father, Romeo Sr., was Tampa's first black officer. Together, we walked beats and patrolled the most dangerous areas of town. Romeo was fearless, except when it came to snakes. Someone was always putting a grass snake in his locker and he would freak out!

WINGS OF FAITH

Badge 146 TPD

I was naive enough to believe that "No one is above the law, and no one is beneath its protection." In the courts, "money talks, the guilty walk" and not all judges are "honorable." People lie under oath and witnesses disappear. Did anyone tell "the whole truth and nothing but the truth" during the O. J. Simpson trial? You be the judge. While attending the Tampa Police Academy, I learned a valuable, but disturbing lesson. One of our guest speakers was a senior judge in Tampa. He was known to frequent gay bars where he often drank too much and he would call for a police cruiser to take him safely home. That is why he felt obligated to teach us how to avoid being found in contempt of court should we appear before him in his courtroom.

"Never argue the verdict!" he began. "There are certain people, who for certain reasons, will NEVER be found guilty in my courtroom, however good your case might be against them!"
"Do your job. I'll do mine and you'll still have a job. Remember these three letters, they will serve you well...CYA-Cover Your Ass!" That was a day I will never forget. There is still corruption within police departments and the judicial system as there is anywhere else in the world. Our nightly news bears that out quite frequently...just look at today's White House!

WINGS OF FAITH

"Not guilty" pleas can be bought and paid for more often than we think. It is rampant in traffic court. For example: while on patrol on Davis Island, a nice section of the city, a lady ran through a stop sign at full speed right in front of me. I gave her a citation to which she replied, "Do you know who I am? Don't you have better things to do with your time?"

I must have heard that a hundred times during my career, but this lady took the cake. She appeared in court with two friends I had never seen before who swore, under oath, that they were riding with her when she was issued the citation and she DID NOT run that stop sign! I replied, "Your honor, if these ladies were riding with her, they were hiding in the trunk!" When the laughter died down in the courtroom (even the judge was grinning), he said, "It's three against one. Majority rules. Not guilty." They left the courtroom smiling, I left biting my lip. Another Tampa judge, rumored to be Mafia connected, was found dead one morning. He had TWO bullet holes in the back of his head...it was ruled a suicide! There was no investigation.

I had a friend on the department who became a detective and was investigating corruption within the department. The day before he was to appear before the Grand Jury, he got a flower delivery at his home. He opened the front door and was gunned down, never to testify in court again.

These things happened many years ago. The department has greatly cleaned up its image and is highly respected today. The great majority of police officers, men and women, are honest, conscientious, and hard working. On the job they "Serve and Protect" to the best of their ability. Because of incidents like Ferguson and Baltimore, all departments are still a work in progress.

81

WINGS OF FAITH

On our Central Park walking beat one night, a 300 pound black female was on her monthly drinking spree and nearly destroyed a bar. She threw bar stools and customers alike from wall to wall. Christine was a "regular." She would spend thirty days in jail for drunk and disorderly, head straight back to a bar and do it again. She was doing life on the installment plan.

With some difficulty, Romeo and I put the cuffs on Christine and called for the paddy wagon. While we were waiting for it to arrive, some militant teens ran through the projects spreading rumors of "police brutality." Within minutes, rocks flew, windows were broken, stores were looted, and fires were set. Any white person in the area was attacked and beaten. Romeo and I escaped the area in the back of the paddy wagon with Christine. The following morning, a sober Christine faced the judge, pleaded guilty and apologized for causing so much trouble. We were cleared of all brutality charges. But the damage had been done. This happened shortly after the Rodney King incident in Los Angeles.

Sometimes comedy and tragedy intertwine within a single day. At TPD, we changed into our uniforms in the locker room. One Valentine's Day, Harry, who was on my squad, was changing into his uniform when we noticed he was wearing silk boxers with large red hearts all over them! His wife had given them to him and promised a romantic dinner if he would wear them to work. He knew he would be teased but he wore them anyway and he was a hit at roll call. Later, on his way home, he was struck head on and declared dead at the scene. I could only imagine what the coroner thought when he saw Harry's silk boxers.

WINGS OF FAITH

Wilma was one of the most interesting "characters" I ever met on my "skid row" beat as a rookie patrolman. At first glance, one saw only the prostitute flitting from bar to bar like a faded butterfly. Her clothes were Salvation Army originals, her hair Miss Clairol blonde, with strands of mousy-brown and gray intermingled. Her age was a mystery depending on whether you counted the years in her life, or the life in her years. Wilma was one of the "regulars" at the jail. She was in and out like a revolving door serving time for shoplifting, drunk and disorderly, and prostitution. The thing people noticed most about her were her tattoos, all roses. The lady was a walking bouquet! She had roses where flowers never grew before.

During one of her sober moments, I asked about her passion for the roses. "When I was a little girl, a hundred years ago," she began, "I lived on a farm in Virginia. Mama had a huge rose garden where I played. It was my favorite place on earth. Then came the divorce, and my family split up. I don't remember much else about my childhood." She sat a moment on the verge of tears and said, "Gentlemen callers don't bring roses to ladies of the evening, so I use their money to buy the tattoos." Tears began to fall as she concluded, "Roses give me comfort. They're the only thing in my life I can hold on to."

Through the years I lost track of Wilma when I went to work at Tampa International, but I heard she was found strangled to death in a cheap rooming house. I wondered if anyone came to her funeral, or if anyone brought roses. She would have liked that. Perhaps then, Wilma could rest in peace.

In 1969, I worked an off-duty job at Tampa's Curtis Hixon Hall. At the time, I thought it was an odd pairing of entertainers - B. B. King and Janis Joplin. B. B. King performed first, and some of his fans departed at the break before Janis came on

83

stage. She immediately worked her rabid fans into a frenzy and encouraged them to come on stage with her, which was not allowed.

When the sergeant in charge of security demanded that fans must return to their seats or the concert would be stopped, an irate Joplin shouted that he could "go f... himself!" In those days there was a city ordinance against public profanity which was a misdemeanor. To have removed her in front of her fans would have caused a riot, possible injuries, and property damage. When "the Rose" came backstage, she was arrested, handcuffed and quickly transported to central booking. She spent a night in jail, paid her fine, and departed the next morning. She told reporters the next time she was arrested, she wanted to share a cell with the Rolling Stones!

Janis Joplin - Arrested in Tampa, FL
for profanity

Another rock icon who was arrested in Florida was Jim Morrison, the lead singer of the Doors. He was arrested for exposing himself during a concert in Dade County. While attending a seminar, I

WINGS OF FAITH

met a police officer who was involved in the arrest of Morrison. I told him about Joplin's arrest in Tampa. We agreed to exchange mug shots. Some officers collect police shoulder patches while others collect mug shots of celebrities. It would amaze you how many V.I.P.'s have been arrested.

There are times when police work can overwhelm you. In Tampa there is a low-lying area where three major streets intersect...Dale Mabry Highway, Henderson Boulevard, and Morrison Avenue. It was at that location one summer afternoon that I wished I was anything but a police officer. It was the curse of "Murphy's Law," - anything that can go wrong will go wrong!

Summer afternoons in Tampa are notorious for severe thunderstorms. It was such a day that I rolled upon a major traffic accident in that intersection. A car had slammed into a utility pole and severed it, all traffic lights were out, electric wires were popping in the street, water was rising, and it was getting dark. I had no backup available and to top it all off, the

WINGS OF FAITH

driver and his female companion had fled the scene on foot. She left her purse and high heels on the floorboard of the passenger's side of the totaled vehicle.

I desperately needed backup to help control six lanes of stalled, irate drivers; the electric company to remove their pole and hot wires from the street; a wrecker and someone to help locate the driver. I "volunteered" some able bodied men to stand out in the rain and lightning to keep cars out of the danger area until help arrived. I was soaked to the bone despite wearing a raincoat. Keeping my paperwork dry was next to impossible. Thank God I didn't need to use the bathroom!

Hours later when the scene was cleared, the driver was located at Tampa General Hospital. He had minor cuts and bruises on his face and sore ribs from hitting the steering wheel (no air bags in those days.) He said his car hydroplaned into the pole and he was dazed. But he managed to walk a few blocks to find a phone booth to call a cab (no cell phones either) to take him to the hospital. He swore he was alone and had no idea how "that woman's" purse and high heels got into his car! I would love to have heard him explaining that one to his wife.

While I was a patrolman with the Tampa Police Department, I came upon a one-car traffic accident in a rural area. The car was upside down and I was afraid it might catch fire. It would take rescue units a while to respond to the scene. Suddenly, out of nowhere, help appeared in the form of an able bodied man who seemed to possess superhuman strength. He helped extract the driver from the car without saying a word. As the sirens from the rescue units grew closer, I turned around to thank the stranger but he was nowhere in sight! There was no car in the area, and no one was seen walking away. The hair on the back of my neck was standing at attention. Sometimes we truly do entertain angels unaware!

Some police officers enjoy sneaking up on cars parked in dark, deserted areas late at night. The sight of people in compromising positions in their cars excites them. To me it was both dangerous and necessary to determine that the female in the car was not being raped, or wasn't a fourteen year old with a thirty something year old man who would call it fake news.

They say "the night has a thousand eyes." It only takes a few to cause life-changing problems. The first rape I investigated happened on prom night. A teenage couple were parked in a dark area by the Hillsborough River to "make out." They didn't notice the car pull up behind them, lights out, with four young males looking for a "good time." They pistol-whipped the boyfriend and left him for dead beside the river. They tore off her prom dress and gang-raped the young virgin. After they had their "good time," they drove away laughing, taking the boyfriends' car keys with them. The frantic girl thought her boyfriend was dead. With no car keys, she ran back to the highway at 2 am, saw my police cruiser coming, and ran naked and bleeding into the street to flag me down. I covered her with a blanket from the trunk of my cruiser, called for backup and an ambulance before locating the crime scene where her boyfriend was in a coma.

Once the parents were notified and the teens were in the hospital, we secured the crime scene until daylight which was a fruitful decision. The four suspects left excellent footprints by the river and fingerprints on the boyfriend's car. Within two weeks, a car matching their description bearing four young males was pulled over on a traffic stop in that area after dark. Their shoes were the same style the rape suspects wore.

WINGS OF FAITH

Tests showed they were exact matches and even had mud in the treads from the riverbank. Fingerprints were also a match. This time, the "good time" was had by my squad!

It has always amazed me how little some people value human life. While I was on patrol one evening, I responded to a "shots fired" call to a redneck bar on the outskirts of town. Upon arrival, I found potential witnesses peeling out of the parking lot. There was a large dead male inside the bar and a bewildered bartender mopping up the blood oozing from three gunshot wounds in the victim's chest.

Blaring from the jute box was a country song, "The Waltz of the Angels" by Wynn Stewart. It kept playing over and over. That turned out to be the reason Amos was dead. In those days you could play three songs for a quarter on the jute box. Amos kept feeding quarters all evening playing the same song. That irritated other patrons in the bar, especially a Barney Fife lookalike known only as Mutt. Mutt asked Amos to let him play something else, an argument ensued, and the bartender stated that Amos struck Mutt with his cane. Mutt ran out of the bar and moments later he returned with a gun, shot Amos three times in the chest then ran out again.

Before the crime scene was processed and Amos was transported to the morgue, another "shots fired" call went out at a bar just a few miles away. At that crime scene, Mutt was the victim, shot six times by Amos' fifteen year old son. Word travels fast in rural areas where everyone knows everyone else. Amos' older son had quickly tracked Mutt to another bar that he was known to frequent. He gave the honor of avenging their father's death to his younger brother, a juvenile, because his punishment would be less severe. I never hear that song anymore, but I'll never forget the irony of it playing over and

88

WINGS OF FAITH

over at a senseless crime scene.

During my time with the Tampa Police Department, there was a police desk within the emergency room at Tampa General Hospital. Officers stationed there would supplement police reports originated by officers in the field. When a crime victim or suspect was sent to the hospital, the officer in the ER would document what type of treatment the person received and if bullets were removed, collect them along with blood-stained clothing for the chain of evidence with that case number.

I witnessed quite a few autopsies during my time there. It was an unpleasant but necessary part of the job. Sometimes a crime victim would walk into the ER, I would originate a crime report and dispatch a field officer to the alleged crime scene to supplement my report. If a rape was involved, a female detective was brought in to conduct the interview and collect the rape kit.

Sometimes there were lighter moments in the ER. One evening an elderly male walked in and appeared to be in great pain with no obvious sign of injury. The elderly gentleman hesitated to tell the admitting nurse why he was there until she took him into a private room. In those days there were no "Depends" or other Velcro type diapers for adults. While changing his cloth diaper, he inadvertently impaled himself with a large safety pin. On the admitting form, under the section where you write the reason for the hospital visit, the nurse wrote "poor penmanship!" It generated some comic relief among the ER nurses who were overworked and underpaid.

On another night, a deceased man was brought into the morgue after falling from the rooftop parking garage at Tampa International. The man had been drinking and wanted to

WINGS OF FAITH

watch airplanes landing on the runways. He climbed over the garage wall and walked unsteadily out onto a helix above the vehicle exit ramp nine stories high. He was enjoying himself and decided to light a cigarette. When he dropped his lighter, he automatically reached for it, forgetting where he was, and tumbled head first onto the shuttle car tracks on the third level where he died instantly. On his hospital report, there was a footnote: "This man proved beyond a reasonable doubt that smoking can be hazardous to your health!"

Working in an emergency room at a major hospital is a beehive of activity as life and death often hang in the balance. I can only imagine the chaos after a mass shooting.

It is sometimes difficult to control your emotions with the horrible sights you see. One evening at twilight time, paramedics brought in a body bag with body parts from a father and son. They had been walking along the side of a road with the son sitting on his father's shoulders. A truck driver heading in the same direction was blinded by the sun and struck them from behind at 40 mph. They never knew what hit them.

Another upsetting incident occurred when a father came home for lunch. Upon leaving his home to return to work, he was running late. He bolted out of his driveway and ran over his four year old son on his tricycle! Both parents nearly lost their minds.

To lose a child is devastating to say the least. When Adam Walsh was abducted from a department store in Florida, only his head was recovered. It nearly killed his parents and nearly destroyed their marriage. Their grief was unbearable for a very long time. Then by the grace of God, John Walsh rose up on the wings of faith and took action. He dedicated

90

WINGS OF FAITH

his life to locating missing children. Through his television show, America's Most Wanted, hundreds of missing children have been found. Sometimes out of the deepest sorrow come blossoms of joy.

A REQUIEM FOR ADAM

Adam's song is a dirge, a haunting refrain,
A senseless rendition of heartache and pain.
Adam's song is an ember that echoes his name
For a cold, wayward zephyr extinguished his flame.
Every note's an enigma; things aren't what they seem,
For the nightmare we share was a pedophile's dream.
Adam's life was a drum roll, a concert of hope...
A crescendo of prayer that allows us to cope.
Adam's melody lingers like a moth to a flame
For out of the ashes God whispered his name.

THERE'S NO SUCH THING AS "CLOSURE"

There's no such thing as closure for those who agonize
When sudden death or tragedy has severed family ties.
There is no heartache anodyne; there is no magic cure.
When your spouse or child is missing, it's painful to endure.
Your friends will offer sympathy but words are hard to say
When your dreams have all been shattered like broken jars of clay.
Until you've walked in that man's shoes, you cannot feel his pain
Or know the emptiness inside that always will remain.
Only time and God bring healing, but nothing is the same...
There's no such thing as closure each time you hear their name.

WINGS OF FAITH

CHAPTER FIVE

AUTOPSY

The morgue is silent, gloomy,
business as usual.
The coroner's scalpel glides
through human flesh
that feels no pain.
Blood trickles onto
a cold metal table.
An electric saw
breaks the silence...
skull is opened like a coconut,
brain removed and weighed,
but yesterday's hero doesn't feel a thing.
Yesterday's hero
dead at twenty-two,
cocaine overdose.
Yesterday's hero
whose future ended yesterday
at a frat party...
Yesterday's hero,
today's headline,
tomorrow's memory.

One of the most atrocious crimes I encountered as a police officer was the rape of a three year old child. The unwed mother left her daughter alone with her boyfriend and when she came home early from work, she found him raping her daughter. She screamed and neighbors called the police.

We arrived at the crime scene; the boyfriend came running out of the house in his bloody underwear. I chased him down and cuffed him. My sergeant, a grandfather, arrived on the scene.

WINGS OF FAITH

He cried when he saw the damage done to the child. Sadly, pedophilia is a crime that often goes unreported because the pervert is a family member.

A short time later, I saw an ad in a magazine showing a teddy bear crying. The Merck ad was warning parents to protect their children against chicken pox. I thought how many times a teddy bear has witnessed a child being abused and was unable to tell anyone so I wrote this poem and it was published in the International Library of Poetry.

TRAGICALLY, ABOUT FORTY CHILDREN DIE EACH YEAR
BECAUSE OF PROBLEMS DUE TO CHICKENPOX.

In 1968, Shirley and I assumed the mortgage on a Tampa home near Tampa International Airport. We were ready to start our family. When nothing happened, Shirley's gynecologist, Dr. Kelleher, examined her and declared she would NEVER have children. He said her tubes were completely blocked and it would be impossible. We applied to The Children's Home to adopt a baby. We were thoroughly investigated and qualified as prospective parents. We both had jobs, a home, and stellar reputations, so we were added to the waiting list.

93

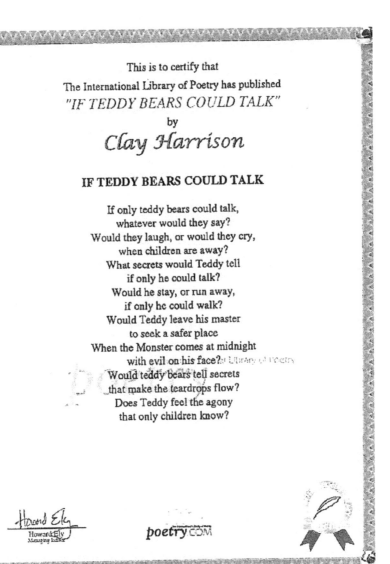

This is to certify that

The International Library of Poetry has published

"IF TEDDY BEARS COULD TALK"

by

Clay Harrison

IF TEDDY BEARS COULD TALK

If only teddy bears could talk,
whatever would they say?
Would they laugh, or would they cry,
when children are away?
What secrets would Teddy tell
if only he could talk?
Would he stay, or run away,
if only he could walk?
Would Teddy leave his master
to seek a safer place
When the Monster comes at midnight
with evil on his face?
Would teddy bears tell secrets
that make the teardrops flow?
Does Teddy feel the agony
that only children know?

Howard Ely
Howard Ely
Managing Editor

poetryCOM

WINGS OF FAITH

Since we were the only ones on the list who had requested a baby girl, we soon became the proud parents of Melanie Anne Harrison in 1969 who was born six weeks earlier. Thank God for women who choose adoption over abortion when faced with an unwanted or unexpected pregnancy. We took Melanie to meet her new grandfather, Shirley's dad, at his job site on our way home. He was overjoyed! Melanie was allergic to every formula but one, Nutramigen, a very expensive one. Our parents took turns buying it to help us out.

Shirley was an adopted child from West Virginia. When the Huddleston's adopted her, she had no earthly possessions except the dirty diaper she was wearing. I'm forever grateful she survived to become my wife.

Me with Melanie

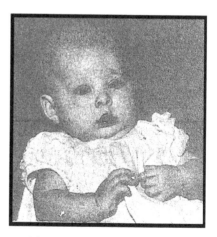

This little doll is Melanie Anne Harrison, age 5 months. She is the daughter of police officer Clay Harrison and his wife, Shirley, of Tampa, FL.

WINGS OF FAITH

GOD MADE THEM ALL

Neither acres of diamonds nor mountains of gold
Can equal the bountiful treasure I hold.
Neither stardust from Heaven nor pearls from the deep,
Can equal my beautiful child fast asleep.
Neither choirs that sing nor roses that bloom,
Can successfully bring such joy to a room.
Neither at sunrise or sunset nor in winter or fall,
Could I ever forget that God made them all!

PRECIOUS CHILD WHO MIGHT HAVE BEEN

O precious child who might have been, we'll never see your toothless grin
Or feel your tender, loving touch that would have warmed our hearts so much.
We'll never hear your hungry cry or see the sparkle in your eye
Because today we come to mourn a precious child who was never born.
You might have been so many things and known the joy that living brings,
But no one offered you a choice and no one heard your silenced voice.
No one cared that you were there and only God could hear your prayer.
O precious child who might have been we'll never see your toothless grin.

To complete our family, we applied to adopt again three years later. During the waiting period, Shirley was having some health issues and thought she might have something serious. Dr. Kelleher examined her, hemmed and hawed, cleared his throat and blurted out, "You're not going to believe this... you're eight weeks pregnant!" She didn't believe him. This was the man who emphatically told her she could NEVER have a baby. She demanded a test. The rabbit died and we were removed from the adoption list. At one of her checkups, her doctor could hear two heartbeats and thought she might be having twins. Thankfully it turned out to be an echo. In her heart, she knew our "miracle baby" would be a boy and she only considered boy's names. The doctor wasn't so sure, and even though he had eight children at home!

On March 2, 1973, Mark Clayton Harrison was born after a long and difficult labor. After twenty-one hours in the birth canal, he arrived with a cone-shaped head full of black hair. He had jaundice and needed to stay in the hospital a few extra days. We were heartbroken going home without him. In contrast, Melanie was born bald. We used to dress her in cute pink outfits and tape pink bows on her head. Everywhere we went, someone would say, "What a cute baby boy!"

We were driving to church one Sunday morning when Mark was three years old. We stopped for a red light and a car stopped beside us. Suddenly Mark shouted out, "Look, Mommy, chocolate people!" Shirley and I wished we were invisible. The black family in the other car laughed, waved, and drove on. Years later, Mark's best friend was an African American boy also named Mark. They derived great pleasure telling people they were the "Marks Brothers!" They said it with a straight face and it garnered them some baffled looks.

When Mark was eight, he was diagnosed with CMT, a form of muscular dystrophy, which Shirley has as well. She had multiple surgeries on her feet from age twelve to nineteen. Mark would be fitted with leg braces with each growth spurt

97

until he was grown. He attended MDA summer camps and years later returned as a counselor. He would have been Mattie Stepanek's counselor, but Mattie died before camp began that year.

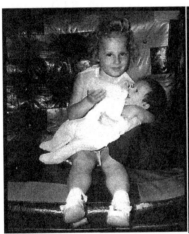 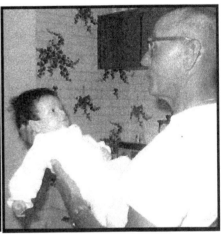

Melanie holding Mark   Shirley's Dad holding Mark

MATTIE

Mattie truly was an angel far wiser than his years.
With broken wings, he could not fly, and left us all in tears.
But he left behind a legacy of "Heartsongs" filled with love
Before leaving us with wings restored for his true home above!

THERE'S SOMETHING ABOUT A BABY

WINGS OF FAITH

CHAPTER FIVE

There's something about a baby that brightens up a room.
For wherever there's a baby, smiles just seem to bloom.
They're the center of attention, that no one can deny...
They're extremely nice to cuddle, especially when they're dry!
They're a heavenly creation made of God's finest clay...
They're a cause for celebration on an ordinary day.
They're the nearest thing to heaven found upon this Earth...
For they're innocent of sin at the moment of their birth.
They're a blessing in a bundle all wrapped in pink or blue
And hands that rock the cradle receive a blessing too.
There's something about a baby too wonderful to describe
And there's nothing like a baby for keeping love alive!

While I was with the Tampa Police Department, we didn't have much money, especially when our children were young. Shirley was a stay-at-home mom at that time. I took any extra jobs I could get, working wrestling matches, concerts, spring training baseball games, even construction jobs with Shirley's father. Sometimes I came home with so much concrete on my jeans they stood up without me in them! I worked with one good-hearted man named Charley who was a real life Mr. Magoo. Once he turned around without looking and knocked me off a scaffold with a 2 x 4. Another time, he nailed his boot to a board and couldn't figure out what to do. I told him, "Unlace your boot, pull your foot out, pull out the nail, and put your boot back on!"

Shirley supplemented our income by babysitting. A lady who worked for the post office and lived near us, needed someone to take care of her little boy when she had to go back to work. Johnny was only 6 weeks old. He was a beautiful baby and we all fell in love with him as though he were one of our own. Our own children just considered him their baby brother. When his

99

WINGS OF FAITH

parents moved away eighteen months later, there were lots of tears. We were heartbroken for a long time.

MOTHER LOVE

More precious than diamonds

Or stars high above

Is the gift God gave us

When He made mother love.

In preschool Mark became good friends with our friend's daughter, Melissa, who also went to our church. She was frequently at our house. When Mark was four years old, he and Melissa, also four years old, were chosen to be Mary and Joseph in a Christmas pageant at Seminole Heights Preschool. They were adorable!

Shirley kept our neighbor's daughter, Tracey, after school while her mother was at work. One day, Shirley stepped inside the door of our bank, leaving Mark and Tracey in the backseat with the A/C running. She gave them strict orders not to move. Moments later, they both appeared at her side and said, "Don't worry, we locked the doors!" Thankfully Shirley's father was only a phone call away and he came to their rescue.

One time while Tracey was at our house, things were too quiet. Shirley went searching to see what they were up to and found Tracey shaving Mark's head with my razor! Things like that are not covered in the "parenting handbook!"

In the 1980's, I published two chap books, "I AM THE CLAY" and TOMORROW'S ANGELS" to raise money for the Jerry Lewis Labor Day Telethon for Muscular Dystrophy. My four dollar chap books raised a thousand dollars! Melanie was a volunteer working the phone bank during the Telethon.

"I Am The Clay" is based on Isaiah 64:8 "O Lord thou art our father; and we are the work of Thy hands." There is also a fine old hymn, "Have Thine Own Way, Lord" based on this scripture and with my name being Clay, it was meant to be!

"Tomorrow's Angels" was inspired by the MDA camps my son attended. Each year some of the previous year's campers had passed away from the most serious forms of muscular dystrophy. Every year at the end of the camp, Christmas was celebrated with Santa arriving on a fire engine. As the

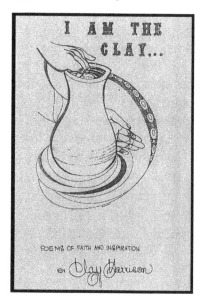

WINGS OF FAITH

campers headed home, everyone wondered if they would be one of tomorrow's angels.

COLORS OF LOVE
(From I Am The Clay)

Imagine a rainbow of black and white,
A moonless sky on a starless night...
Picture a sunrise, a colorless sun,
Pale Autumn leaves when Summer's done...
Envision a garden dreary and gray,
Lackluster roses in a bridal bouquet...
How boring and dismal God's earth would be
Without any color for our eyes to see!
He paints every sunrise after the storm,
Bright flowers each Spring when earth is warm,
And there on His canvas in Heaven above,
He paints every sunrise with colors of love!

My friend, Yankee owner George Steinbrenner, a Tampa resident, bought a box of books from me to pass out at his Bay Harbor Inn. "The boss" often gave Mark Yankee souvenirs. Years later, Mark interned with the team during spring training while he was studying for a degree in sports medicine at the University of South Florida. Mr. Steinbrenner was a generous man.

When George found out I was approaching retirement, he asked if I was interested in working security in the Yankee organization. I was greatly honored, but my plans were already made. Shirley would not be happy if I changed my mind about moving to Virginia. Her heart was set on having four seasons

102

WINGS OF FAITH

each year.

A LION'S HEART

I can't fight his battles or win his victories,
It breaks my heart to see him robbed by his disease.
There beats a lion's heart in a body frail and thin,
And if courage played a part my son would always win.
He scores the winning touchdown in Dreamland every night,
And fights like Rocky every foe before the morning light.
I can't fight his battles although I feel his pain,
So I'm content to love him and we neither one complain.
Despite growing up with muscular dystrophy, Mark always dreamed
of being an athlete. He was able to play on a youth soccer league
championship team, Blackwatch. He was too slow to be a starter, but he
truly enjoyed every moment he was on the field.

When Tampa was awarded a pro football team, the Buccaneers, Mark took to the team like a duck to water! We spent hours each week getting autographs and photos from every player and buying every souvenir he found. Many players gave him their wrist bands and the equipment manager gave him footballs. The owner, Hugh Culverhouse, gave me a Buccaneer wrist watch and a small digital desk calendar for Mark. We went to every game that first season even though they lost every one! Later on, he even played catch with his favorite quarterback Doug Williams.

Frank Ross, who was a photographer for the team, noticed how much Mark loved talking football with the players. He wrote a story about Mark, calling him the Little Buc-A-Roo and it was published in the Tampa Bay Pro Football Report. Needless to say, Mark was thrilled.

LITTLE BUC-A-ROO

Wide-eyed with excitement, he tumbles into bed.
With his energy all spent, he bows his sleepy head.
The Bucs won a thriller, and his dreams came true.
The game was an up-hiller for my little Buc-A-Roo.
He's somewhere in Slumberland, reliving every play.
With Doug's chin strap in his hand, he dreams of Tampa Bay.
He's running for a touchdown, instead of counting sheep.
Little Buc-A-Roo of Tampa town, is smiling fast asleep.

During spring training baseball season, Mark's favorite teams were the New York Yankees and the Los Angeles Dodgers. We would get autographs and Mark started collecting wristbands (with team logos) from the players. Some players even had their picture on them. He still has every one he ever received. We made an annual trip to Vero Beach each spring to Dodger Town and Mark got to be batboy one time. When the Yankees moved their spring training from Ft. Lauderdale to Tampa, Mark was studying sports medicine at USF and interned with the team while Derek Jeter was with the Tampa Yankees. Mark helped the players warm up, gave them massages, and drove them to their hotel and to doctor appointments.

When we went to see visiting football and soccer teams at their hotels, Melanie came with us. She loved to help get autographs and have her picture taken with the players. Several times, players from visiting soccer teams came to our house and played soccer with Mark and Melanie in our backyard. The players were very generous, often giving them soccer balls, jerseys and other souvenirs from their team. They both have nice collections today.

National's Park Father's Day 2012

These were wonderful experiences for Mark and Melanie's childhood, but the most enduring was with the New York Cosmos soccer team. Our home team was the Tampa Bay Rowdies, but Mark fell in love with the Cosmos, especially their great forward, Giorgio Chinaglia.

Each time the Cosmos were in Tampa, we visited them at their hotel. A friendship developed that has lasted a lifetime. Mark was allowed to ride on the team bus and had a field pass. It was like he became the team mascot.

He was given autographed soccer balls, but the biggest thrill

105

came when Giorgio gave him his jersey following a game. After the North American Soccer League disbanded, we remained friends.

When Giorgio passed away unexpectedly, Mark went to his funeral and read a poem I wrote for the occasion. Mark became friends with the family and other team members. They correspond and visit to this day.

Giorgio Chinaglia giving his Cosmos' jersey to Mark

Mark visiting Giorgio at his home

GIORGIO

WINGS OF FAITH

He was kind as he was talented to all who came his way,
A legend on the soccer field to all who saw him play.
He earned respect among his peers for he gave the game his all
And there was great expectation each time he had the ball.
He loved the game he played so well and felt it in his soul.
For he could make a scissors kick with his back to the goal.
He was a striker on a mission wherever he would play,
And how deeply we shall miss him now that he's gone away.
As much as Giorgio loved the game, he loved his family more.
His smile could brighten any room when he walked through the door.
He was a friend to all who knew him, much more than that to me,
For he inspired one crippled child to be the best he could be!

WINGS OF FAITH

CHAPTER 6

TAMPA INTERNATIONAL AIRPORT POLICE

"And the peace of God which passeth all understanding, shall keep your hearts and minds through Christ Jesus."
Colossians 4:7 NIV

After five years of service with the Tampa Police Department, I turned in badge 146 and went to work at Tampa International Airport, a city within a city, that had just established their own police department. Airport security had come of age and they investigated every crime under the sun, and then some, with threats to aircraft and VIP protection. They also patrolled the WWII Drew Field property that surrounds the airport. I became badge 132 for the next twenty-seven years and collected my pension in 1999.

WINGS OF FAITH

CHAPTER SIX

During my career there I made many good friends and met and protected many famous people. I wrote hundreds of poems for employee's birthdays, anniversaries, funerals, and retirements. The most unusual was for a female officer who was getting married who asked me to write the wedding vows in poetic fashion on a poster. When I gave it to her, she asked if I would like to attend the wedding. Since it was being held at Lake Como, a nudist colony, I declined the invitation.

A skycap, Herbert Myers, loved my poetry so much that each time I gave him a Salesian book he would memorize it in a few days. While on a flight to Philadelphia to attend a wedding, the lady who was sitting in the seat beside him said "You have to read this poem!" It was one of mine. Herbert pulled out his autographed copy of the same book and told her that we were friends. She was so amazed that two people from different parts of the country were touched by the same poem and happened to sit beside each other on the same flight to Philadelphia. God does work in mysterious ways!

Many years later, after we moved to Williamsburg, we were invited to a New Year's Eve party at the home of Pastor Bill Howard and his wife, Lou. Pastor Bill was a retired Disciples of Christ pastor and she was an elder at Olive Branch. I gave her one of my Salesian books and she was so excited to show me that she had been receiving these little books for many years. She told me she had often used my poems for devotions as I was her favorite poet. Then she told me something I will never forget. She said, "I knew you before I met you." We immediately became great friends and I wrote a celebration of life poem for her when she passed away.

109

WINGS OF FAITH

CHAPTER SIX

THE MAN BEHIND THE BADGE

When I pass by, some only see my badge and uniform,
Someone they fear when speeding, a lighthouse in the storm.
I swore to risk my life for you, to always "do or die,"
But it's guilt by association when cops steal or lie.
I go places you won't go, see crimes that make me cry,
It's never business as usual when I go speeding by.
I work nights and holidays, then sit in court all day
While deals are made, people lie and the guilty walk away.
No one ever calls me hero...but lots of other names!
With pride, I take it all in stride and every day's the same.
I serve, protect, and do my best in all I'm called to do
For I'm the man behind the badge who's always there for you!

During the Gulf War, I frequently worked security details for General Schwartzkopf, a Tampa resident, as he traveled back and forth. I gave him my current Salesian books and one day I received a nice letter and an autographed photo from him.

I wish the American people felt that way about our troops who served during the Vietnam era. Once again the General's letter is living proof about the power of poetry, even on the battlefield.

WINGS OF FAITH

October 7, 1991

Dear Mr. Harrison,

Thank you very much for your kind words and the book of poetry. As you may have guessed, I enjoy reading poetry. It relaxes me, so after a stressful day, and I've had many lately, I like to put my feet up in my chair and read a poem or two.

Let me assure you there was no place I would have rather been than leading America's finest in Operations Desert Shield and Desert Storm. The pride and professionalism our sons and daughters displayed in the performance of their duties was truly inspiring. I could not have been prouder of them.

Again, thank you for the poetry collection. Remember, you and the American people gave the troops in the Middle East strength through the knowledge that their country was fully behind them.

Sincerely,

H. NORMAN SCHWARZKOPF
General, U.S. Army, Retired

In November, 1972, I wrote a poem, One World Under God" for the Apollo 17 astronauts, Eugene A. Cernan, Ron Evans, and Jack Schmitt after Frank Borman received criticism for quoting from the scriptures while in orbit.

111

WINGS OF FAITH

I wrote the poem on a 60 foot scroll and got about 3,000 signatures on it supporting our space program. I started with the mayor of Tampa, Dick Greco, the Tampa City Council, the University of Tampa football team, and passengers from around the globe who passed through Tampa International Airport that month. After their flight, I received a thank you letter from Apollo 17 Commander Cernan.

ONE WORLD UNDER GOD

Modern science and technology have improved the human race.
And men of high morality are exploring outer space.
It's more than personal or national pride that guides each Astronaut –
It's faith that God is on their side, and courage which prayers have wrought.
Their mission isn't one of conquest as they explore the Heavens above;
Nor an international contest but a labor of Brotherly Love.
Astronauts Cernan, Schmitt and Evans soon will depart this earthly sod.
May their voyage throughout the Heavens proclaim, One World Under God!

WINGS OF FAITH

NATIONAL AERONAUTICS AND SPACE ADMINISTRATION
LYNDON B. JOHNSON SPACE CENTER
HOUSTON, TEXAS 77058

APR 2 8 1973

REPLY TO
ATTN OF: CB

Mr. Clay Harrison
6412 N. Clark Avenue
Tampa, FL 33614

Dear Mr. Harrison:

What excitement your lengthy, congratulatory message caused in our
office! We had it on display all of one day in our mail room office
and everyone had the opportunity to look it over. It is great. We
are planning to find a permanent place for it in our Astronaut Library.
It is a remarkable accomplishment and we are indeed most grateful for
the many well wishes and messages of good cheer from all three thousand people.

We are enclosing some pictures which we took on the Apollo 17 mission
and have added some of the exceptionally good pictures from some of
the other flights for you, and many, many thanks for your tremendously
superb greeting card!

Sincerely,

Eugene A. Cernan
Captain, USN
NASA Astronaut

Ronald E. Evans
Captain, USN
NASA Astronaut

Harrison H. Schmitt
NASA Astronaut

Enclosure

I imagine I have blushed more times in a courtroom than any
police officer in history. I grew up where a curse word was
never heard or tolerated. Mom would not allow it and woe to
him who dared to take the Lord's name in vain!

When an officer testifies in court, you must say, word for word,
what was said at the crime scene and what a suspect said

when he or she was arrested. It can get vile in a hurry. Each time I had to repeat such language, I blushed. I didn't even like having to write such words in my reports. It was a necessary evil.

My most embarrassing moment in court came one day while I was waiting on the front bench to testify in a DUI case. The bailiff brought in the female prisoners for trial when one of the "ladies of the evening" shouted out, "Hi, Clay! I didn't know you were a cop!" That caused a few snickers among the other officers on the bench. She was a prostitute who had been in my graduating class at Jefferson High School. I would never have recognized her. She looked like she had aged twenty years since high school. That was a sad day.

My most embarrassing moment on duty came at the 22nd Street Projects in Tampa, a high crime area. My rookie partner dropped me off to use the restroom at a convenience store. Before I walked through the door, we received a "shots fired" call. My partner yelled for me, "We've gotta go!"

Before I could get back into the cruiser, the car started rolling. I had to dive through the window on the passenger side, headfirst. We peeled out with my feet sticking out the window at sixty miles an hour. With siren wailing and red lights flashing, we amused the onlookers. It turned out to be a false alarm!

During the Watergate investigation, I was teaching a Sunday school class for fifth graders at Oak Grove United Methodist Church. I wanted the class to show support for our president and our country. On a small poster I wrote a poem on the front and had each child write a message to President Nixon stating that they were praying for him and asking God to bless the U.S.A. A few weeks later we received a thank you letter from President Nixon and an autographed photo. They were framed and on display at the church for years.

THE WHITE HOUSE

WASHINGTON

June 21, 1974

Dear Mr. Harrison:

There is nothing more heartening to me than the goodwill and faith expressed by you and so many other citizens throughout our Nation. I want you to know how deeply grateful I am for the prayers and good-will of all who joined in signing this special card.

With my appreciation and best wishes,

Sincerely,

Richard Nixon

WINGS OF FAITH

Since my days in California, I have enjoyed the company of nuns. I admire and respect the tireless work they do. One afternoon I encountered Sister Mary Rinaldi, a Salesian nun, as her vehicle was about to be impounded because she had left it unattended in a "loading only" zone at the airport. Sister Mary was a fund raiser for the Salesian Mission Charities headquartered in New Jersey. Since I had been donating my poetry to the Salesian Inspirational books for many years, we became friends immediately.

Sister Mary was staying with the nuns at St. Joseph's Catholic School in Tampa. She invited me to speak to the children at the school while she was in town and it was there that I met Sister Isabel, the principal. She also enjoyed my poetry and invited me to teach poetry appreciation classes at the school. The Catholic schools in Tampa had an annual poetry competition where twelve poems were chosen to represent each month on a calendar for the following year. Several St. Joseph students' poetry was included in the calendar that year. Each time a new Salesian book arrived, Sister Isabel read my poems to the student assembly in the mornings.

Sister Mary was instrumental in raising funds to build a retirement home for elderly nuns in New Jersey. Her Adopt-A-Nun campaign was inspired by a blind man who had a vision that people could adopt a nun by making monthly donations in their name. The Sister would, in turn, keep that person in their daily prayers. Shirley and I adopted Sister Mary and Sister Isabel immediately. The retirement home was built and I am proud that we had a small part in that effort.

WINGS OF FAITH

Sister Mary Rinaldi

Sister Isabel Garza

With most jobs, a person has a pretty good idea of what to expect on the job on any given day. The routine is very much the same. When a police officer puts on the uniform and goes to work, you can expect the unexpected. When you think you've seen it all, you haven't! I cited some of those incidents in my CHAPTER about the Tampa Police Department.

There were plenty of bomb threats called in, usually by passengers who missed their flight, and VIP protection was a common occurrence, especially during the Gulf War and Tampa's two Super Bowls. We were always looking for fugitives and runaways. There were some nasty domestic disputes and dozens of suicidal people who decided to jump from the ninth floor parking garage. Many times I ended up being the report writer and sketch artist for my squad.

Our one constant duty was traffic control in the arrival and departure levels. Many flights are delayed due to inclement weather or mechanical issues. This creates a major problem, especially during peak times. When flights are delayed, drivers

117

WINGS OF FAITH

who are picking up or dropping off passengers don't want to park in the garages and wait it out. When they get a parking ticket, or get towed, some get irate to the point of violence.

It requires great patience and restraint to endure hours of angry drivers circling the building calling you names for enforcing the no-parking signs in loading zones. It gets really bad during the holidays. Several people wrote nasty letters to the newspaper one year and my response was printed in the paper.

With millions of people arriving and departing TIA each year, you never knew what the next call would be. At any given moment a flight can land with a medical emergency, a baby being born, a rock band having a food fight, or passengers fighting aboard the plane. Planes have skidded off runways or landed on taxiways by mistake. When the landing gears malfunction, the fire department foams the runways and lots of prayers are said. Inside the terminal, there are always irate passengers when flights are cancelled or delayed for hours, or custody disputes become violent. Homeless people, runaways, fugitives and mentally ill people show up at any given time. Because of the diversity of the traveling public, there is often the need for interpreters. People fall down escalators, get stuck in elevators, and children get lost. All of these incidents require a mountain of paperwork. If a juvenile is involved, it doubles.

VIP protection requires working hand in hand with other agencies. When Air Force One is on the ground, the Airport Police guard it while it is unattended. Elvis' Lisa Marie plane would sometimes arrive and depart in the middle of the night and the public would never know he had been in town. Many celebrities travel on customized buses after arriving at the airport. We had holding areas for those people and I saw many through the years. One day Porter Wagoner took me on his tour bus to meet Dolly Parton. I saw her without her wig. She gave Porter a look that could kill!

One day an artist named Amy was on the transfer level sketching caricatures of passengers and employees as part of a craft fair. I was working that level and during a lull, she asked me to pose for her, free of charge. She was a Christian and noticed there was no chapel in the airport where people could pray and meditate between flights. I had been suggesting that to the Aviation Authority for years. It finally came to fruition before I retired.

WINGS OF FAITH

In 1990, I sent Mother Teresa a poem called, "The Saint Of Calcutta." Her love for the lepers and orphans was amazing. She offered hope to the "poorest of the poor." I was surprised when she took the time to reply to me. Mother Teresa is truly a saint now and I am honored that for one brief moment in time she knew my name.

THE SAINT OF CALCUTTA

For Mother Teresa

She's the saint of Calcutta who labors night and day
To comfort the sick and dying and take their pain away.
She seeks no fame, no glory, she's there to serve the Lord,
And when she gets to heaven great will be her reward.
She makes the world a better place with her unending love
For those who have no place to go but to the Lord above.
She dries their tears; she calms their fears and prays they will not die
Until they have met the Master as time keeps ticking by.
She's the saint of Calcutta, a servant of the Lord,
And when she gets to heaven, great will be her reward!

MISSIONARIES OF CHARITY
54A A.J.C. BOSE ROAD
CALCUTTA — 700016

Dec 22, 1990

Dear Clay Harrison,

I am grateful to you for your prayers for
me and thank you for the beautiful poem
you have written.

God has indeed given you the gift of expressing your thoughts beautifully in poetry. More
important than that, he has given the gift to
discover what is beautiful, pure and noble
and the capacity to love. Use all these gifts
He has given you to draw others to God and
so make your life something beautiful for Him
- holy - for this you have been created -
to be holy.

Let us ask Our Lady to give Jesus to us and
to help us to keep Him always in our hearts
through humility, love and compassion.

May the love, the peace and the joy that Jesus,
Mary and Joseph shared in the Holy Family fill
your hearts at Christmas and throughout the
coming year. God's blessings on you in 1991 !

God bless you

le Teresa mc

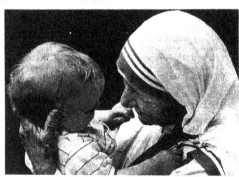

MAKE US worthy, Lord
to serve our fellow men
throughout the world
who live and die in po-
verty and hunger.
GIVE THEM, through our
hands, this day their daily bread; and by our un-
derstanding love, give
peace and joy.

God bless you
le Teresa mc

PRINTED AS A GIFT TO THE MISSIONARIES OF CHARITY
BY THE KNIGHTS OF COLUMBUS

WINGS OF FAITH

Princess Diana was killed in a traffic accident in Paris the same week that Mother Teresa passed away. The circumstances surrounding Diana's accident dominated the news for a long time and generated many conspiracy theories. She was adored worldwide and her premature death was a great loss. Her compassion and generosity will not be forgotten.

THE "PEOPLE'S PRINCESS"

Her candle burned at both ends and made a lovely sight,
But too soon it was extinguished one dark Parisian night.
Her smile held the masses captive, a priceless work of art.
Now that smile is frozen on the canvas of the heart.
All mankind sent her flowers and watered them with tears,
For her legacy of caring will last a thousand years.
She touched us with her kindness and set our hearts aglow.
She belongs now to the ages in heaven and earth below.
She was the "People's Princess," an angel taking flight.
Her candle burned at both ends and made a lovely light!

OCTOBER MIRACLE
Jessica McClure, Baby in the Well
18 months old, Midland, Texas

"Line the streets with people,
Ring church bells one and all –
Baby Jessica's in the well!"

WINGS OF FAITH

We held our breath; we said a prayer and watched a tragedy unfold.
She was so young, so very small, and not yet two years old.
"She's still alive!" a fireman said. Millions shed a happy tear
To hear her sing a nursery rhyme amid such gloom and fear.
Perhaps she'll live; perhaps she'll die there in the mud and slime
And still she had the will to sing while passing precious time.
We held our breath; we said a prayer when the third day came around
Awaiting her resurrection from that muddy Texas ground.
Bells rang out from the steeple proclaiming, "All is well!
The streets were lined with people with a miracle to tell!

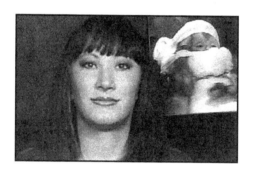

The last five years of my career at Tampa International, I worked the graveyard shift, 11:00 pm to 7:00 am. For the most part, it was quiet and peaceful except for bad weather delays when the terminal was filled with anxious passengers and relatives.

While on patrol most nights, I often listened to, "Music Through The Night," hosted by Mike Kellogg on the Moody Broadcasting Network. Mike played Christian music, read scriptures, and heartwarming stories. We corresponded often and he read my

WINGS OF FAITH

Salesian poems on the air. I don't know how many listeners Mike had in the wee hours of the morning, but all who listened were blessed.

Dear Clay:

Greetings from the Moody Broadcasting Network!

Thank you for your wonderful letter and uplifting words to MUSIC THRU THE NIGHT. It was an honor hearing from you and I'm glad to have you as part of our listener family! I enjoy hearing you tell about your life as a patrolman. Sorry you won't be able to listen for a while. I'll miss having you Clay, but it's nice to know that you are out there sharing the Good News with a lost world. Thanks for the quote from Longfellow, I'm honored.

My continued prayer for you, good friend, is that you would walk closely with God and remain as faithful to Him as you are today.. We trust you will listen and be blessed in a special way as the words and music refresh your soul and draw you even closer to the Almighty One. God bless You as He continues to do a good work in you! (Col 1: 10, 11)

Sincerely,
Mike Kellogg
MK/lb

When I was Evangelism Chairman at Oak Grove United Methodist Church in Tampa, our associate pastor asked me to accompany him on a visit to a shut-in who had just come home from the hospital. Mary greeted us with this, "I've just returned from Heaven; it is wonderful!" She gave us a detailed account of passing through a tunnel with angelic beings into a glorious white light. She saw colors not seen here on earth, and heard music so beautiful she didn't want it to end.

Suddenly she remembered Henry. He was her special needs son. She had never filed legal papers that would insure Henry would be taken care of following her death. This is why she had summoned us to her bedside. Mary said her spiritual hosts allowed her to return to earth after she had been declared DOA at the hospital. When she cried out from her body bag, it created quite a stir in the morgue! We assisted Mary in getting her legal affairs in order, and three days later, she returned to heaven.

Once I began working the midnight shift on a regular basis, I became known as the Midnight Writer. I was chosen to be chaplain of the Fraternal Order of Police, so I became the Walter Jones of my department. When someone got out of line or messed up on the job, I wrote a Midnight Writer poem that would appear on our bulletin board.

I referred to the airport as Whoville (with apologies to Dr. Seuss) and police officers as the Whos. Supervisors were the big Whos and the chief was the great Who. Each Who was identified by their badge number. I was Who 132, etc. There were over one hundred Midnight Writer poems written the last five years of my career. I used good natured humor to point out situations that needed to be corrected. The poems were well received with few exceptions by Whos who really messed up. Sometimes humor is the best medicine.

WINGS OF FAITH

WHOVILLE COPS

Whoville cops are underrated for the tireless job they do.
They're on the job both night and day risking their lives for you.
They keep the shuttled masses safe – it's always been that way.
You'll find whos waiting to serve you when you visit T.I.A.

WHOVILLE COPS NEVER DIE
(Free at Last: March 26, 1999)

Whoville cops never die - some just look that way.
Too much stress wears you down and your hair turns gray.
All too soon, your feet are flat and your hearing starts to go.
Your eyesight's next, so what the heck if your waistline starts to grow!
Big whos here and big whos there, tell you what to do.
But they can't agree on anything so, friend, it's up to you!
"Big Brother" whos are out there too, so be careful what you say.
Be P-O-L-I-T-I-C-A-L-L-Y C-O-R-R-E-C-T or you may have to pay.
My hourglass ran out of sand so now I must retire
And pass the torch so younger whos can set whoville on fire.
But if some day, someone should say, "Where's that old who, Clay?"
Just smile and say, "Old whos not dead; he only looks that way!"

TALES FROM WHOVILLE

WHOVILLE POLICE DEPT.

TALL TALES AND
SHORT LIES JUST FOR
FUN FROM THE PEN
OF THE MIDNIGHT
WRITER

126

WINGS OF FAITH

In high stress jobs like police work or firefighting, there is a need for comic relief. Every department has one or more practical jokers. At Tampa International, A.K.A. Whoville, our practical joker was a real life Elmer Fudd look-alike named Fred. Sometimes, he went a little too far to get a laugh. In our breakroom, across from the employee's cafeteria, we had a microwave oven and a refrigerator for those who brought their lunch. One day I had a container of cherry Jello for my snack. I placed it on the table where Fred was sitting and reading a newspaper. I put some whipped cream on the top and was returning the whipped cream to the refrigerator when I glimpsed him wadding up newspaper into a ball and putting it on top of the whipped cream. Immediately the newsprint bled black stripes down the cream to my Jello.

I walked back to the table, looked at my ruined Jell-O, and looked at Fred who refused to make eye contact with me. Without saying one word, I picked up the Jell-O and dumped it on top of his bald head! He couldn't stand up as it would have spilled red Jell-O all over his uniform. He sat there in shock, crying out, "It's so cold, it's so cold!" Other officers scurried to bring paper towels to remove my snack from Fred's head as I walked out of the room. I expected to be called into the Chief's office for a reprimand, but it never came. That time Fred's joke backfired and the joke (or Jell-O) was on him! The day he retired, Fred shook my hand and said he'd never forget me anytime he saw red Jell-O.

There are multiple parking garages and rental car areas at Tampa International. It's Nirvana for car thieves. It's also a choice place to abandon stolen cars and catch a flight. Once in a while we recovered cars that had been abandoned with a dead body in the trunk, usually from a drug deal that had gone bad. We also encountered snakes in parking garages where

127

WINGS OF FAITH

they took shelter on cold nights. It kept us on our toes when on patrol in the garages.

On a quiet night, I got a call from the FAA in Tampa tower about an intruder with large red eyes on a runway. The intruder was a twelve foot alligator! I was used to stray dogs on the runways and flocks of birds, but this was a first for me. I called for backup and we used ropes from the trunks of our cruisers to carefully lasso both ends of the gator. We tied it to some 2x4's brought to us from the maintenance garage.

During the process, the police helicopter hovered above putting a spotlight on the gator. The chopper got too close, the gator stood erect and hissed at the officer holding the spotlight, and he almost fell out of the chopper. It's amazing how fast gators are on land. The gator was transported to the maintenance garage where it was picked up by wildlife officers the following morning.

I first met Muhammad Ali shortly after he adopted Islam as his religion and changed his name. He was in the "I am the greatest!" time of his life. He came to Tampa to train in a small gym close to Jefferson High School. I told him my name was Clay and I was a poet. He looked me over and said, "You may be a better poet, but I'm better looking!" I wasn't about to argue with him. He was born on January 17, the same day as Shirley.

In later years, when he was battling Parkinson's disease, he came to Tampa promoting Muhammad Ali cookies. He sat at a table for hours autographing cookie bags. His most endearing image was lighting the Olympic flame in Atlanta in 1996.

I had a chance encounter with author Alex Haley while he was

128

on a book tour for Roots. He was staying at the Airport Marriott and he came to the coffee shop on the transfer level after midnight while I was on duty. I recognized him immediately. I got his autograph and we had a brief discussion about the horrors of slavery and the importance of names and one's ancestry.

Millions call themselves Christians, but politics get in the way. People are labeled conservative or liberal, right wing or left wing, and we are divided into many denominations. Our actions should be based on WWJD (what would Jesus do?) in any given situation. I don't believe Jesus would malign others with hateful emails during an election or participate in a smear campaign against those who have a different point of view. Didn't Jesus command that we love one another? Do we not pledge to forgive those who trespass against us each time we pray the Lord's Prayer? Too many times we build walls that divide us instead of bridges that unite us.

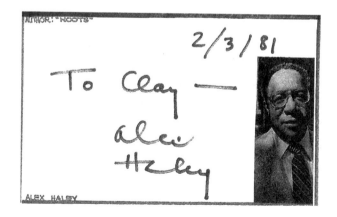

WINGS OF FAITH

During my career at Tampa International I had the pleasure of meeting or corresponding with some stalwarts of the Civil Rights Movement. I greatly respect those who have fought for civil rights. I had the honor of escorting Coretta Scott King to her flight when she was in Tampa for a speaking engagement and she was gracious and humble in every way.

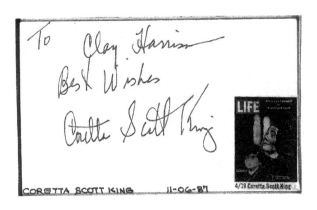

In 1989, Malcolm X's daughter, Attallah Shabaz, brought her group Sweet Honey In The Rock to do a concert in St. Petersburg and I assisted them with parking and loading their equipment. I received a kind thank you letter and an autographed photo from them.

WINGS OF FAITH

Philmore High School

Class of Yesteryear

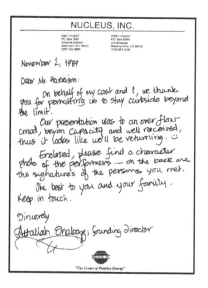

WINGS OF FAITH

I corresponded with director Spike Lee while he was filming the movie, Malcolm X. He responded with a letter about making the movie.

FORTY ACRES AND A MULE FILMWORKS · SPIKE LEE

4ο⎤α

July 25,1991

Dear Clay:

Thank you for the letter of support that you sent to me. It was greatly appreciated. It's nice to know that I have fans that care so much!

As you can imagine, pre-production on my latest film, Malcolm X is keeping me very busy, but I think it will be well worth the effort. I believe Malcolm X will be my best film ever!

Again, thanks for all of your support.

Sincerely,

Spike Lee
Filmmaker

SL/sp

WINGS OF FAITH

I also corresponded with Rosa Parks several times through the years. She sent me letters and a biographical sketch for my collection.

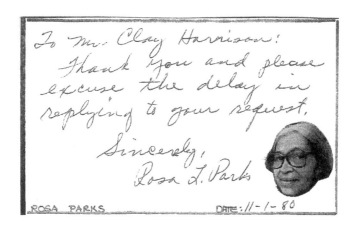

To Mr. Clay Harrison:
Thank you and please excuse the delay in replying to your request.
Sincerely,
Rosa L. Parks

ROSA PARKS   DATE: 11-1-80

```
ROSA L. PARKS
c /o Elaine Steele
Executive Assistant
9311 Wildemere Ave.
Detroit, Michigan 48206

January 18, 1991

Dear Mr. Harrison:

     Thank you for your kind words of encouragement.
Please continue your interest and enthusiasm about my
work and the work of many other positive individuals.

     The enclosed information is a brief biographical
sketch and a list of research materials about some of
my involvement.  I hope they will be helpful to you.


                Love, Peace and Prosperity,

                Rosa L. Parks

                Rosa L. Parks
```

WINGS OF FAITH

CHAPTER SIX

I had a nice visit with Jesse Owens in his hotel room when he was in Tampa speaking to youth groups. His focus was teaching young black men to concentrate on sports instead of joining gangs.

THE TRAILBLAZER

From impoverished Alabama to Berlin's Olympic gold,
He became an instant hero in headlines big and bold.
He achieved more than medals – for with dignity and grace,
He won hope and admiration for all the Negro race.
He proved black men could compete when all was said and done,
For he was not content to be a raisin in the sun.
Jesse Owens led the way in life as on the track
And proved to all that Brotherhood is neither white nor black.

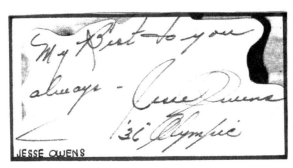

Jesse Owens *Setting national track-and-field records in high school and world records in college, this sharecropper's son mocked Hitler's boasts of Aryan superiority by capturing four gold medals in the 1936 Berlin Olympics.*

134

WINGS OF FAITH

Before the Billy Graham Crusade that changed my life in 1958, I had a few minutes with Ethel Waters before she sang His Eye Is On The Sparrow. She was going blind at that time. She felt my face and asked me if I knew her "sweet Jesus" and gave me a big hug. It warmed my heart.

I attended a Maya Angelou poetry reading at the University of South Florida. Years later she sent me an autographed copy of her inaugural poem, On The Pulse Of The Morning. She was one of my favorite poets and she is greatly missed.

135

WINGS OF FAITH

History was made on January 20, 2009, when Barack Obama was inaugurated as the 44th President of the United States. Martin's dream took a giant step forward! He inherited a country on the brink of disaster and left office eight years later with the country in much better shape, with no scandals on his watch.

THE IMPOSSIBLE DREAM

*With mutual respect they came to celebrate and see
A dream fulfilled before their eyes that once could never be.
With joyful hearts, thousands came to witness history,
Huddled masses filled with hope and possibility.
Around the world, all nations watched the impossible come true
And tears flowed like rivers before the day was through.
It was a gathering of eagles and lowly sparrows too,
A time of change and jubilation, a time to start anew.
Thousands came and millions watched on this cold winter's day
As history has recorded and shall not pass away.
A dream deferred was realized upon this hallowed sod,
A dream that showed the entire world "One Nation Under God."*

Written while watching the inauguration
of President Barack Obama 01-20-09

CHAPTER SIX

THE WHITE HOUSE

WASHINGTON

January 16, 2017

Dear Clay:

One of the most important things I've done as President is read messages from Americans like you. And whether you sat down to write me a letter back in 2009 or just last week, I wanted to say thank you for writing.

Letters like yours have given me the chance to hear the real stories that make up the ever-changing narrative of America. They are stories of your setbacks and successes, your fears and your hopes not just for today—but for the country and the world we'll leave to our children and our grandchildren. I want you to know that I was listening. I heard your stories. And you made me a better President.

In 2014, a young mom took a chance and shared her family's story with me. She said she knew that "*staying silent about what you see and what needs changing never makes any difference.*" She was right. And so, while serving you has been the greatest privilege of my life, I want you to know that when I leave the White House, I'll still hold the most important title of all: that of citizen.

And as a proud American citizen, I believe that we are a constant work in progress. Our success has never been certain. None of our journey has been preordained. There's always been a gap between our highest ideals and the reality we witness every day. But what makes us exceptional—what makes us Americans—is that we have fought wars, and passed laws, and reformed systems, and organized unions, and staged protests, and launched mighty movements to close that gap. To bring the promise and the practice of America into closer alignment. To form that more perfect union.

So our collective future depends on our collective willingness to uphold our duties as citizens: to vote, to speak out, and to stand up for others knowing that each of us is only here because somebody, somewhere, stood up for us. And for the rest of my days, I promise I will be right there alongside you, continuing to do my part to build a better, more prosperous, more diverse and inclusive America—an America with a future full of hope.

From all of us in the Obama family—thank you for writing.

All the best,

WINGS OF FAITH

Airport Police Officers are also first responders. There is a fire station on airport property, but police officers are first to render first aid at this city within a city.

An elderly passenger had a heart attack one day while in line at a ticket counter. I was first on the scene and initiated CPR on the gentleman, a German citizen. After a few stressful minutes, his wife tapped me on the shoulder and said, "Sir, you can stop now. The angels have taken him away!" She said she saw two angels take him up through the ceiling and disappear. He had indeed flat lined and was gone when the paramedics arrived.

The wife showed an amazing calm demeanor under the circumstances. The peaceful look on her husband's face assured her there was nothing to fear. She couldn't understand that we hadn't seen the angels.

Bob Tucker was the most conscientious and dedicated police officer I worked with at Tampa International. He truly lived up to our motto, "To serve and protect" and "justice for all." Bob was extremely allergic to insect bites. He got into a bed of ants one weekend and coded in the ER. When he returned to work, Bob told me while he was in the hospital and they were frantically working to resuscitate him, he left his body on the table and floated around the ceiling watching everything they did to him and heard everything they said. Once he was stabilized and back in his body, the ER Doctor was astonished when Bob gave him a detailed account of what was done to him. He said the experience removed all fear of dying from him.

On December 31, 1972, baseball immortal, Roberto Clemente, was killed in a plane crash delivering hurricane relief items to

138

Nicaragua. During the baseball season that year, he belted his 300th hit, securing his place in baseball's hall of fame. He also secured his place in the humanitarian hall of fame.

I was at work at Tampa International the day the news broke about his tragic death. I encountered a wrestling superstar I had known for years and asked if he had heard the news about Clemente. He looked me in the eye and said, "So what, he's just another dead n.....!" That unexpected reply left me speechless. I had no idea a pro athlete could be so cold and heartless about the death of another athlete.

Three weeks later on a foggy night, a small plane crashed into Tampa Bay. Three of the plane's four occupants, all wrestlers, died in that crash. The pilot who died that night was the very wrestler who made that racial slur about Roberto Clemente!

On January 8, 1995, I suffered a heart attack while raking leaves. It felt like a fireball was burning its way through my chest, and it wouldn't go away. Shirley called our family doctor and he told her to get me to the hospital ASAP, but he forgot to tell her to call "911". She put me in the car and raced to St. Joseph's Hospital, a few miles from our home.

I was clammy and "gray-looking" when we arrived at the Emergency Room entrance where help was waiting. They started an IV and began cutting away my clothes as they rolled me into the ER. All I could say was "thank God Mom always told me to wear clean underwear!" It cracked everyone up in the waiting room. That was one of Mom's three Golden Rules. The other two were, "Be kind to everyone," and "Always respect women and your elders." Mom would be proud of the "Me, Too!" movement in our country today.

WINGS OF FAITH

A Cardiac Catheterization revealed that I had four completely blocked arteries. I had never been hospitalized before, had no prior symptoms, therefore had no idea anything was wrong. In layman' terms, my body had produced too much bad cholesterol and not enough of the good kind. Surgery was scheduled and I was given a 50% chance of survival. My surgeon was a former classmate from Jefferson High School. Prior to, and following my six hour operation, I felt the "peace that passes all understanding." I knew in my heart that God was in control and whatever happened, He would watch over my family. My spiritual journey was at a crossroad, but I was sheltered beneath the wings of faith.

Following the surgery, my nurse Janell, treated me like a rag doll. I had just been wired back together, had a twenty-five inch incision running up my left leg, and could not raise my head off my pillow after it hung off the operating table for those six hours. I had multiple tubes coming out of my body. It wasn't a pretty sight! Because of the rough treatment from my nurse, when I was able, I wrote her a poem, "Janell, The Nurse From Hell!" She thought it was great and showed it to everyone.

I didn't know until later how many people had been praying for me. A Mass was said for me at a Catholic church, prayers were said at a Jewish Temple, a mosque, and four different Protestant churches! It's no wonder I felt such peace. God is awesome!

WINGS OF FAITH

SURVIVOR!

The heart attack could have killed me that January day –
A fireball burning in my chest that would not go away.
I had a "fifty-fifty" chance, the doctors said to me.
Four blocked arteries laid me low when I was fifty-three.
A quad bypass was in order – it was a stressful time.
My faith was being tested with mountains I must climb.
Cards and prayers came pouring in from near and far away.
I was prepared to meet my fate whatever came my way.
A peace that passes understanding came over me that day –
Five hours in surgery and I emerged okay.
Twenty-three years have come and gone – I treasure every one
Since that day when I bowed my head and prayed, "Thy will be done."

Following my quad bypass surgery, I went through six weeks of rehab at St. Joseph's Hospital. It was exhausting but I felt really good after each session. One of the cardiac patients in my group was a comedian, Buddy Graff, who was co-starring in a musical revue with Mickey Rooney at the Showboat Dinner Theater in St. Petersburg at the time.

Graduation - Cardiac Rehab

Clay and Buddy

WINGS OF FAITH

Buddy and I quickly became friends. He would push me on the exercise equipment, motivating me to go all out in order to get in shape so I could return to work. To celebrate completing cardiac rehab, Buddy treated Shirley and me to front row seats to see him perform with Mickey Rooney. It was a fun evening I'll never forget. Due to Buddy's travels across the country, I lost track of him through the years. I pray that his heart surgery was as successful as mine has been.

Since childhood when my mother planted seeds in Maxwell House coffee cans, I have loved gardening. I plant just about everything that will grow in my zone, and frequently garden for my friends. After all, are we not stewards of God's creation?

While we lived in Tampa, Shirley worked at Scrap-All, Inc. Her boss' father, Charlie Wax, was deeply saddened after his wife passed away. He would often sit and visit with Shirley when he came to see his son, Herb. Charlie noticed that there were always fresh-cut flowers on Shirley's desk. One day he asked where she got them and he was amazed when she told him, "from our yard." She invited him to come and see our garden. He came and it changed his life!

Charlie Wax in his garden

WINGS OF FAITH

Charlie had often stated that he had nothing to live for anymore without his wife. He was overwhelmed by the beauty of our flowers so I offered to help him grow flowers in his yard. Charlie lived in a retirement mobile home park. Within a year, his yard was a showplace. When we stopped at garden centers, we always bought something for Charlie. He loved plants that were easy to propagate so he could give cuttings to his neighbors. He always had plants to give away, and he couldn't wait to wake up each day and check on those plants. We even had a calendar made for him called, "Charlie's Garden," complete with color pictures of his garden.

THANK GOD FOR FLOWERS

Thank God for flowers of every hue
from baby pink roses to plumbago blue
The fragrance of Jasmine enhances the night,
and each water lily is a pearly delight.
Magnolias by moonlight bring sweet memories as
springtime awakens the blossoming trees
The common hibiscus brings uncommon joy
and shy violets are bashful and coy.
Long-stemmed red roses are reasons to sing,
and the frost-covered crocus usher in Spring.
Lavender orchids decorate the prom,
and pastel carnations pay tribute to Mom.
Flowers bring comfort to pauper and King,
for one cannot measure the pleasure they bring.
From Easter-white lilies to plumbago blue,
thank God for flowers of every hue!

143

WINGS OF FAITH

CHAPTER SIX

How can anyone walk through a garden or a field of wildflowers and not believe in God? Man may hybridize, but he did not create flowers that grow in places where no feet have trod. He did not place within an acorn the possibility of a mighty oak tree, or place within a field of clover the nectar that bees will convert to honey. Man may have walked on the moon, but "only God can make a tree," as poet Joyce Kilmer once stated.

YOU'RE NEVER ALONE IN THE GARDEN

You're never alone in the garden. Tiny eyes are always there
Watching, waiting for you to leave a crumb for them to share.
The trees are filled with singing birds, perhaps a squirrel or two,
While frogs and rabbits in the brush watch everything you do.
God's creation comes alive with creatures great and small,
And the farmer and the gardener respect them one and all.
The garden's a sanctuary for all who linger there
For peace abides and hope abounds even when the trees are bare.
You're never alone in the garden; you'll meet God's creatures there,
And when you least expect it...perhaps angels unaware!

I have given away thousands of the Salesian inspirational books throughout the years. Many pass them on to others like ripples in a steam. A Jamaican lady at a flea market we visited in Tampa passed my books to a senior citizen, Celo Chapman, who wanted to meet me. Shirley and I went to her home and we became great friends. We took her out to eat, she cooked for us, and I gardened for her until we moved away in 1999.

Celo was a set decorator in Hollywood until she married a diplomat and lived in Europe before World War II brought them

WINGS OF FAITH

back to the states. Once she became a widow, she moved into a cottage behind her daughter's home in Tampa. It was Celo who named our home in Williamsburg, CEDARLOVE. She said it was made of cedar and it would be filled with love once we moved in. The cedar has now been replaced, but our CEDARLOVE sign still hangs over our front door.

When Celo turned 100, I adapted a Bill Gaither song, "There's Something About That Name,"...to "Celo, Celo, Celo, there's just something about that name," etc. She was thrilled"

Celo's eyes have seen the glory of one hundred passing years.
There's a fire that burns within her that's stronger than her fears.
Celo's faith is a lighthouse when storms of life appear.
Her smile outshines the rainbow whenever she is near.
Celo's eyes have seen the world change in many different ways
From the "Gilded Age," two World Wars, to our space program today.
Celo's life has been a blessing to everyone she knows.
She leaves behind fond memories everywhere she goes.
Celo's eye reflect a love light she so graciously shares
With her family and friends and everyone in her prayers.
Her sweet, sweet spirit warms us with laughter and some tears
As we celebrate her birthday...a mere one hundred years!

WINGS OF FAITH

CHAPTER SIX

WELCOME HOME

When our faith journey is over and we are laid to rest,
We shall behold Him face to face for we are surely blessed!
We'll meet in the clouds somewhere and nevermore shall roam
When God wraps his arms around us and says, "Welcome Home!"

When I returned to work at TIA after cardiac rehab, I had to pass a rigid physical and run a mile in less than ten minutes. That was a piece of cake for me. One of our officers was extremely overweight. He was put on a strenuous exercise program and had a fatal heart attack driving home from work one afternoon.

At the time of my heart attack, I weighed 220 pounds, the heaviest I had ever been. After
rehab, I had lost 20 pounds and felt really good.

I outlasted four police chiefs during my career at the airport. I was number one in seniority my last five years. I had first pick of shifts and days off which allowed me to have weekends off so I could go to church. Family time to me was precious. I enjoyed working the streets and investigating crimes. I never had to shoot anyone and no one shot at me. I never wrote an undeserved traffic ticket or used excessive force on anyone. By treating everyone fairly, I had very few resisting arrest cases. I even got a few thank you's from people I arrested.

After three years as an Army MP during the Vietnam era, five years with the Tampa Police Department, and twenty-seven years at Tampa International, I had enough and headed for

WINGS OF FAITH

the serenity of Williamsburg where we have four seasons (sometimes in the same month!) and I can grow spring bulbs, enjoy autumn leaves, and shovel a little snow.

Shirley and her mother had already travelled to Williamsburg and found a house with an in-law suite for Shirley's parents. They had sold their Tampa home years before and moved in with us after our children married and moved out. We put our house on the market and hit the road.

WINGS OF FAITH

CHAPTER 7

RETIREMENT

*"To everything there is a season,
and a time for every purpose under heaven.
" Ecclesiastes 3:1 NIV*

Mount Pilatus, Lucerne, Switzerland

When Shirley and I first started planning for our retirement, Fripp Island, South Carolina, was our first choice. Shirley had relatives there and we had visited them several times. One year, Shirley, Mark, and her parents visited near Christmas. Shirley and Mark had a great time riding around in her uncle's enclosed golf cart playing Christmas music on a cassette player and experiencing a meteor shower by the sea wall. The

WINGS OF FAITH

island is only about three miles long and they had a good time riding the golf cart from one end to the other and seeing all the beautiful Christmas decorations.

Fripp Island is located on the coast near Beaufort and across from Hilton Head Island. Much of the movie, "The Prince of Tides" was filmed there. The author of the book, Pat Conroy, also made his home on the island. After the war scenes were filmed and the explosions created craters, a golf course was built turning those craters into sand traps! Alligators are common visitors on the greens and golfers generously allow them to play through! Shirley and Mark had a close encounter with a young alligator on one of the walking paths on the golf course. Shirley stopped the cart and they patiently waited for the gator to saunter across in front of them and continue on his way. She promptly turned the cart around and got out of there! The homes on the island are beautiful but the many herds of deer consider gardens their salad bars. Dolphins are a common sight along the sea walls. On our last day there, two dolphins backed up to the wall and flipped their tails as if they were waving goodbye to us.

The downside to living on Fripp Island is the one and only bridge to and from the mainland often washes out in hurricane season leaving the residents stranded unless they have a boat. We had our fair share of hurricanes living in Tampa for forty years so we settled on our second choice, Williamsburg, Virginia.

When Shirley and I "retired" in 1999, we moved to Williamsburg with Shirley's parents in tow. Although we downsized, it took two trips back and forth to get everything moved. My best friend at TIA, Ken, helped us load the moving truck. He was a good partner.

149

WINGS OF FAITH

After moving dozens of times as a child when my parents lived from payday to payday, I came to hate moving! Every time we moved we had to downsize. With each move I lost things I wanted to keep...toys, baseball cards, comic books, etc.

I dislike moving even more than I dread spring cleaning when we rearrange things in the house. For weeks I can't seem to find anything. The women in my life must all have the moving genes. My mother cleaned and mopped daily because we didn't own the house. She moved things around quite often.

Shirley's mother made slipcovers to give old things a new look, and was forever wall papering. When we were first married and had very little furniture, Shirley rearranged things while I was at work. Not good! While working the evening shift, I came home at midnight. I undressed in the dark and sat down on the bed – only it wasn't there anymore. I landed in the floor with a thud and I was not happy. I bruised more than my ego that night. I try not to curse but...

There was an ice storm prior to our moving in and trees were down in our yard. I spent many hours digging flower beds and landscaping the yard. I had to learn what to plant in the mid-Atlantic area compared to the tropical gardens I had in Tampa.

We visited several churches before we found our church family at Olive Branch Christian Church, Disciples of Christ. We felt at home the moment we walked through the door. An interim pastor, Rev. Diane Snowa, was just starting there. We bonded with her immediately.

WINGS OF FAITH

SHE CAME TO US A STRANGER
For Pastor Diane Snowa
(From a grateful congregation at Olive Branch Christian Church)

She came to us a stranger
and quickly won our hearts,
Our thoughts turn melancholy
now that our friend departs.

She comforted and hugged us
and wiped away our tears,
Encouraged us to have faith
that's stronger than our fears.

She taught our children how to pray
for Jesus loves them too.
She blessed our pets and kissed a pig...
is there nothing she won't do?

She gave the best she had to give
and did it all with love
Because her heart overflows
with blessings from above.

She came to us a stranger
with grace that faith imparts.
The memories are golden
she leaves within our hearts!

 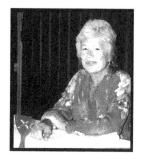

WINGS OF FAITH

If everyone had a Pastor Bill in their life the world would be a better place. He served thirty years in the Navy, saw active duty in World War II, and Korea. He served as a Navy Chaplain from 1957-1960, and then taught psychology at Old Dominion University for 25 years.

Pastor Bill served as our interim minister at Olive Branch Christian Church from 1994-1995 and maintained his membership there until his death in 2013. He was a never-ending source of anecdotes, a walking encyclopedia of scripture (chapter and verse), master chef of corn-on-the-cob, and a devotee of "dessert first" at church dinners.

Despite all of his degrees and titles, he insisted that "just plain Bill" would do in addressing him. He was the kind of pastor that other pastors confided in.

Bill created a Monday morning prayer group at Olive Branch

November 11, 2012

Olive Branch Christian Church
(Disciples of Christ)
7643 Richmond Road
Williamsburg, VA 23188

that continues today and the church library was named in his honor. He also helped create a Christian Businessmen's Luncheon which I attended with him, and I had the pleasure of driving him to the weekly prayer meetings. As Bill descended into his "Golden Years," his driving became "notorious" and riding with him became quite an adventure. Surely he had guardian angels riding with him. I wrote the following poem for him at his Minister Emeritus Service.

152

WINGS OF FAITH

"PASTOR BILL"
for
Curtis William Howard, III
Minister Emeritus: 11-11-12

Pastor Bill's a testimonial
To what God's love can do,
His life has been a ministry
Of humble service, too.
In times of sorrow, Bill is there
To lend a helping hand,
And when our hearts are breaking
He helps us understand.

Bill's an ultimate prayer warrior
Who always keep in touch
With his Lord and Heavenly Father
He loves so very much.
He can quote you the scriptures;
They're written on his heart,
And when Bill's faith is truly tested,
It becomes a work of art!

Bill's God's "energizer bunny"
But his battery is low,
Still he's sowing seeds of kindness
Wherever he may go.
He has no "retirement" plans
Until his race is run,
And someday at life's finish line
God tells him, "Bill, well done!"

Clay Harrison

WINGS OF FAITH

Our current pastor at Olive Branch is Rev. Richard Cline, a spirit-filled man who is an inspiration to us all. He has been our pastor for eight years now. His thought provoking sermons like, "Snake on a Stick," have a unique way of getting his message across. Many of his sermons inspire me to write a poem.

He's there in a heartbeat when someone is in the hospital. His compassion and love for his congregation is truly outstanding. He has a marvelous sense of humor which puts people at ease. We love to tease him about his North Carolina accent. We often tell him he cannot retire or leave our church until all of us have moved on to our heavenly home!

Shirley has worked at Our Saviour's for eighteen years, the past seven plus for Pastor James Nickols. He has worked to make many major improvements to an aged church and it is beautiful. He is a rare and generous man. Shirley tells him he is paying the congregation to be their pastor because he does so much from his own pocket. His love for God and the congregation is something to behold.

Pastor Nickols met his wife Janell when he was a Navy chaplain. Also a pastor, Janell recently retired as a school teacher. Pastor Nickols has also retired and they plan to enjoy their retirement and do some long awaited travelling.

WINGS OF FAITH

The highlight of our retirement came in 2001 when we took our belated honeymoon to Europe. We toured Germany, Italy, Austria, and Switzerland. We accompanied a group of seniors from Lafayette High School along with several couples from our church.

We flew into Frankfurt, Germany, where our tour bus and guide were waiting for us. We departed for Rothenberg, the Middle Ages walled city, where we spent our first night after a brief tour of the city. The next morning was Easter Monday which is a holiday in Europe. It had snowed during the night. I got up early, walked the wall around the city, and made a pile of snowballs and put them by our bus. When everyone started boarding the bus, I told them the snowballs were our German Easter eggs.

We rode the Romantic Highway and made a lunch stop in Munich. Since it was a holiday, most of the shops and markets were closed. We were able to enjoy watching the Glockenspiel go through its movements at noon in the plaza.

After lunch in Munich, we proceeded to the Dachau Concentration Camp. It is located within a charming German village. It is painful to imagine the horrors and atrocities that transpired within those walls of the camp. Surely the villagers heard the screams and gunshots and smelled the human flesh being cremated beyond those walls daily. But, what could civilians do against the Nazi troops next door?

We saw the gas chambers where the female prisoners thought they were going to get a shower. We saw the rows of ovens with the gallows above them where the Jews were hanged and cremated along with the roll call square where prisoners were shot daily. There were a few remaining barracks where

WINGS OF FAITH

prisoners were tortured and raped. There is a memorial garden which contains a mass grave of the bodies of one thousand unidentified Jews. This was a lot for all of us to take in and it created a somber mood as we boarded our bus to continue our trip.

Dachau Entrance

Krematorium

THOUGHTS ON VIEWING DACHAU

In a lovely German village, behind an iron gate,
There stands a concentration camp, a monument to hate.
The barracks have been demolished but the ovens still remain,
And the prison within a prison that wrought in human pain.
There's a sign upon the rafters where prisoners were hanged,
And a sculpture on the killing field where murders were arranged.
A mass grave in the garden there pays tribute to the dead
Behind the "Krematorium" where Hitler's plan was fed.
In that lovely German village, there's a morbid irony –
The sign upon the iron gate states, "Work shall make one free!"

WINGS OF FAITH

CHAPTER SEVEN

GARDEN OF EVIL

"Man's inhumanity to man makes countless thousands mourn!" Robert Burns

In a pristine German village the natives call Dachau,
Screams that once flowed from there are eerily silent now.
The past can't erase the memories still blowing in the wind.
Such memories are just too painful for hearts to ever mend.
The stench from the Krematorium no longer fouls the air.
Puddles of blood in roll call square no longer linger there.
Tall poplar trees that saw it all bore witness, but cannot tell
Of evils that made the death camp a truly living hell.
Within a brick gas chamber, women said a final prayer.
Now a prisoners' memorial has been erected there.
On these grounds there is a garden, but buried beneath the sod
Are the bodies of a thousand Jews known only unto God!

As we entered the Bavarian Alps, the scenery was incredibly beautiful. Perched between two mountain peaks was "Mad King Ludwig's" fairytale castle, Neuschwanstein. It is an extremely popular tourist destination and it was the inspiration for Cinderella's Castle at Disneyland. King Ludwig's second castle, Hohenschwangau, is located on another mountain peak a short distance away.

Access to Neuschwanstein is by horse-drawn carriages. However, they only take you part of the way up the mountain side. You must walk the last quarter of a mile. Some people were able to walk the entire way. Shirley rode and I walked. The Byzantine style palace offered a splendid view of the Bavarian Alps. The palace itself staggers the imagination.

157

As our journey continued, we passed through the Dolomite Mountains and arrived at a lovely resort area on the Aegean Sea. Unfortunately, we were subjected to the work of thieves. Since we were running late for our dinner, we were directed into the dining room and told to leave our luggage unattended. After dinner, it was discovered that an expensive camera had vanished from a suitcase. Naturally, no one saw anything.

In the middle of the night, a fire alarm erupted and a voice came over the intercom directing everyone to come down stairs to the lobby immediately and to leave our doors open. We chose to ignore that statement and locked our door. Those who left their doors open found items missing upon returning to their rooms. Again, hotel employees had no idea what happened.

Early the next morning, some angry Americans boarded a boat to go to Venice and spend the day. We toured the Basilica San Marco and the Murano Glass Factory. We were taken on a guided tour of the Doge's Palace, crossed the Bridge of Sighs, and entered the dungeon where countless Italians died.

We ate pizza and gelato beside the Grand Canal and walked across the Rialto Bridge which spans the Canal. Some took Gondola rides through the smaller canals. Shirley and I explored some lovely gardens away from the main plaza until it was time to board our boat and head back to the hotel. There were no incidents that night, as far as we know.

The next morning, we headed for Verona. Upon arrival, we discovered that it too was a walled city. Huge wisteria plants were growing through cracks that spread far and wide in the ancient wall. A large, functioning arena is located in the heart of the city and there are many statues and beautiful fountains.

WINGS OF FAITH

The "must see" area of Verona is a crowded courtyard where the fictional balcony scene from Romeo and Juliet is alleged to have happened. Below the balcony is a gold statue of Juliet where people are encouraged to rub her bare breast for good luck. I declined.

While the tourists' focus is on rubbing her bare breast, the pickpockets have a field day! One lady in our group had her wallet and passport stolen from her backpack. She did not realize it until much later.

We made a stop in Innsbruck, Austria, in the province of Tirol, on our way to Lucerne, Switzerland. As we crossed the bridge over the River Inn, the view took our breath away. Although it was quite cold, the Royal Gardens were in full bloom. The main attraction was Emperor Maximillian's Golden Roof which overlooks the main street. It has been widely photographed. Our visit was brief; we had two hours to eat, shop, and get back aboard our bus to continue the journey.

That evening, we arrived at the Hotel Roessli Alpenachstadt in Lucerne. It had snowed that day, yet there were beautiful red tulips blooming in the flower beds. Across the road from the hotel was a beautiful chalet. Shirley took photos of it and when we returned home, she had one enlarged and framed it. She fell in love with Lucerne and Innsbruck and jokingly told me to go home, sell everything, and come back so we could live there! It was here that our fellow traveler discovered her wallet and passport had been stolen. Before the trip began, we were told to make a copy of our passports in case this happened. She and her husband had to take the train to the American Embassy in Bern and missed one whole day of our trip.

159

WINGS OF FAITH

After a wonderful breakfast the following morning, we crossed the historic Kapell Bridge to see a world famous sculpture, the Dying Lion Monument, a tribute to the Swiss Guard. The weather went from raining to sleeting. It didn't seem to bother the dozens of swans in the river below. Swans seemed to be everywhere in Europe.

Our next stop was Mt. Pilatus. We rode cable cars to the top of the mountain. We were in whiteout conditions and could barely see the Hotel Rigi-Kulin located there. Icicles taller than us were hanging from the roof. Legend has it that a large red dragon resides in the ice caves atop Mt. Pilatus. We took their word for it and didn't stray too far into those caves. Coming back down from the mountain, we were given baseball caps with a red dragon on them as a souvenir.

THE DYING LION OF LUCERNE

I stood speechless in April rain and felt the lion's dying pain.
Upon his shield, his paw was laid protecting it from death's refrain.
As hope and strength began to fade, he laid there dying, unafraid.
A broken lance had pierced his heart yet he seemed indifferent to the blade.
He lies there for the world to see the Swiss Guard's role in history,
A dying lion made of stone forever carved in antiquity.
The lion monument was erected to the memory of
26 Swiss Guard officers slain in Paris in 1792".

WINGS OF FAITH

On our way back to Germany, we drove beside the Rhine River and passed Europe's largest waterfall, Rhine Falls. We stopped to purchase clocks and souvenirs at a shop that sold the beautiful German Cuckoo Clocks in the Black Forest. They call it the Black Forest due to the density of the ancient trees located there. However, a severe storm had passed through the area recently and many of those wonderful trees were on the ground.

Our final stop was at Heidelberg Castle on a mountain overlooking a beautiful river and Heidelberg University, Germany's oldest university Again, it was another rainy day. The world's largest wine barrel is located on the lowest level of the Castle. For many years German citizens paid their taxes with wine. Now, tourists can buy wine there with a label bearing their name.

As this was the last day of our tour, we were encouraged to spend any German money we had on hand. This was previous to the Euro. We had to exchange money at each border crossing. Our tour bus delivered us to the Heidelberg Castle at the top of the mountain. However, when our tour of the castle was complete, we had to walk back down the mountain. Some of the ladies needed a pit stop before walking down in the rain. When they entered the ladies' room, a "sumo-sized" German man was sitting at a table collecting money before they were allowed to use the facilities. Shirley gave him all the German coins she had left and he told her "Not enough!" That did not set well with her so she promptly told him he should be ashamed of himself, sitting in a ladies restroom and turning ladies away. She also told him that we do not treat people this way in America! It was a slow and delicate walk back down to the town where a McDonald's came to the rescue!

WINGS OF FAITH

On the flight home we were given a bottle of French champagne for our belated honeymoon. Since we do not drink, we gave it to a lady named Paulette at our church and she was thrilled. She was an actress in France as a young woman. At my surprise 60th birthday party, she came up to me and said, "Let me give you your first French kiss!" After a moment of silence, the room erupted in laughter, and Paulette blushed when she realized what she had said.

9-11: A Day That Time Stood Still

September 11, 2001, like December 7, 1941, is a day that will live in infamy! The events of that day had everyone glued to their televisions and brought our nation to its knees. It was a major wake-up call, a loss of innocence. We believed it could not happen here...but it did.

Like ripples in a stream, the sorrow spread around the world. A river of tears were shed, but we bonded as Americans because

WINGS OF FAITH

we had a common enemy...Al-Qaeda. We didn't think of ourselves as Red states or Blue states. Ordinary citizens became heroes beside courageous first responders. Some died rescuing others; many would die years later as a result of breathing harmful elements in the air. We will never take our precious freedoms for granted again. God bless the U.S.A.!

AMERICAN MOURNING

We hug a little longer now our loved ones every day
Aware that all the things we love can quickly pass away.
From time to time we shed a tear and take more time to pray
Since terror struck us from the skies and changed our lives that day.
We wave Old Glory higher now to honor those who died,
And pledge allegiance one and all with reverence and pride.
We're stronger, more united now, than we have been before,
A nation of unsung heroes gathered at Freedom's door.
Our fighting men and women have ventured in harm's way
While others protect our home front since that September day.
We hug a little longer now remembering the lost,
For Freedom endures forever and today we count the cost.

GOD WAS THERE!

"Where was God?" some have asked when the twin towers fell,
And the Pentagon was burning like the fiery gates of Hell!
Where was God in Pennsylvania when Beamer yelled "Let's roll!"
On a day we'll long remember that is etched within our soul?
God was there in both the towers; He was there on every plane.
He was there in Pennsylvania to minimize their pain.
He was there at the Pentagon and He heard every prayer,
And although He was so busy no one saw Him there.
He was there with the firemen and all who helped that day,
With the truckers and the workers who cleared debris away.
On September the eleventh, many had a cross to bear.
And thousands felt His presence for surely He was there!

GROUND ZERO, 2003

We go there to remember a loved one or a friend
Who perished there two years ago like ashes in the wind.
Ground Zero now is holy ground where great twin towers stood
And life will never be the same in this New York neighborhood.
Some lay flowers here and there, some gather rocks and sand,
Mementos of the way things were before terrorists struck our land.
Children come to read the names of those who died that day,
A potpourri of humanity that touched us all some way.

WINGS OF FAITH

THE GRAVEYARD OF SHATTERED DREAMS

In lower Manhattan, twin towers stood
Until hijacked planes fell from the sky
On a September morning bright and good
And two years later we're still asking, "Why?"
Why did our loved ones have to die that day
Leaving shattered dreams in a concrete grave?
How could cowardly men hate us this way
In the "home of the free and the land of the brave?"
Will historians write that we did our best
To fight the "good fight" since that fatal day?
Will history say that we passed the test
Because of the faith we exhibit today?
Our dreams were shattered that September morn,
But out of the ashes are new dreams born!

"HAVE YOU SEEN MY DADDY?"

Inspired by words on a missing person's poster
on a New York building showing a father holding his son.
Have you seen my Daddy? He's missing today,
And Mommy said angels came to take him away.
If you find my Daddy wherever you roam,
Please tell him we miss him and need him at home.

WINGS OF FAITH

Mr. Clay Harrison

THE WHITE HOUSE

Thank you for your letter. In these difficult days especially, the President and I draw strength and comfort from your words and prayers.

September 11, 2001 was a day of unspeakable tragedy and sorrow, and our world changed forever. But America's spirit is stronger and our hearts are more united thanks to the countless acts of heroism, compassion, and courage that continue throughout the country and around the world. Americans have much to be proud of and confident about — our Nation is strong, the government decisive, our people resilient, and the military determined.

We hope in the coming months and years that you will remember and support those who bear the greatest burden: the injured, the bereaved, the Nation's children, and now the members of the military who will make us proud, as always, by defending our freedoms.

Laura Bush

GEORGE BUSH

July 27, 2005

Dear Clay,

Just a quick note of thanks for the collection of your songs, "Lest We Forget." I appreciate your sharing your music with me. The songs are a great way to remember our veterans and honor our Armed Forces. And certainly, British Prime Minister Tony Blair and our own President Bush deserve praise for their leadership roles in the war against terror.

With my best wishes,

G. Bush

By the grace of God, Shirley and I have faced, and survived, life-threatening illnesses. Prior to the 2006 holidays, Shirley was diagnosed with stage three, HR2 positive breast cancer, one of the most aggressive forms of breast cancer. With the chemo available at that time, she had a 25% survival rate. While she was receiving chemo for four months and then radiation treatments for six weeks, Dr. Dennis Slaymon at UCLA Medical Center finally got approval to release Herceptin, increasing her chance of survival to 75%! Timing truly is everything!

Following her mastectomy, I sat by her bed throughout the night. I prayed, cried, and wrote her thirteen poems while she slept. Shirley had prayed there would be no severe pain. There was none. She never took one pain pill. Three days later, she was back at her desk at Our Saviour's Lutheran Church with drainage tubes hidden under her clothes. I never saw her bitter or depressed, and never once did she ask, "Why me, Lord?"

Shirley too was bathed in prayer and get well cards flooded in, plus crocheted butterflies and quite a few angels that still keep watch on the mantle above our fireplace.

Prior to her mastectomy, Shirley had been scheduled for foot surgery due to her muscular dystrophy. That surgery too was a success. A few weeks in a wheelchair and she was good to go. In a six week period, she had four different surgeries. Her spirit was amazing!

Shirley was diagnosed with arthritis when she was thirty-eight years old. Her right knee cartilage was destroyed by arthritis. She fell on an icy gangplank in Salzburg, Austria during a Christmas cruise in 2008. A year later, she finally faced the fact that the knee had to be replaced. She should get "frequent flyer" status at hospitals!

167

WINGS OF FAITH

FOR SHIRLEY

Last night I sat beside your bed and prayed throughout the night
That God would ease your suffering and send a healing light.
Our prayers have not been answered in ways we understand
And tears fell on your pillow as I caressed your hand.
They cut away your cancer but said it could return,
And while I watched you sleeping, my heart began to burn.
For forty years I have loved you; it hurt to see you cry,
For should I ever lose you, the world I know would die.
You're my Alpha and Omega, my beginning and my end.
You're my soul mate and my lover, my ever present best friend.
We'll get through this together God willing, you and I,
For we pledged our love forever and love can never die!

Shirley's oncologist, Dr. Mark Ellis, was highly loved and respected in Virginia and beyond. He survived brain cancer while in college. The treatments he underwent were so vile; he decided to dedicate his life to making things better for other cancer patients.

Dr. Ellis hugged his patients and treated them like family. He was an encourager to the nth degree and did everything possible to make them feel as comfortable as possible. He was also a musician and a huge Beatles fan. For his birthday, I gave him an autographed photo of Ringo Starr and he was overjoyed. It would be his last birthday. During a vacation, he injured his back. His cancer had returned and he died a few months later. I wrote a tribute poem for him, but mere words seemed insufficient to honor such a beloved man. He was so excited when Shirley completed her two years of chemo and radiation. He told her to live her life to the fullest as he lived his.

TEN THOUSAND HUGS

(In loving memory of Dr. Mark Ellis)
His smile launched ten thousand hugs for those who passed his way.
His heart overflowed with love for those he touched each day.
Compassion was his trademark for he had been there too,
And through it all, he kept the faith that somehow gets us through.
He was a man who shared his dreams of a better life for you.
He tried always to do his best to make our dreams come true.
Mark had his share of sorrows but there were victories too;
We were blessed to have known him and share his point of view;
To live each day with gratitude and hope that springs anew
Remembering each day the things that cancer cannot do!
We'll miss his hugs and warming smile but we must say, "Adieu"
And celebrate a life well lived and praise the man we knew!

WINGS OF FAITH

There are things we can't wish away that we must meet head on
When we must face reality and sometimes stand alone.
When the doctor says, "It's cancer!" your heart begins to break
And deep inside you're hoping that there was some mistake.
No one wants to hear those words but sadly, many do,
And because it is what it is, it is now up to you.
There will be a time of testing like none you've ever known,
But when you win the battle you'll find that you have grown.
Many will pray and cheer you on but you must run the race,
And you can cross the finish line with dignity and grace.
It is what it is; that's true, but God still answers prayer,
And when you cross the finish line He will meet you there!

RELAY FOR LIFE 2014

We walk to honor loved ones and friends who've passed away,
For survivors and each patient who gathers here today.
Sweet memories of our loved ones warm our hearts each day.
With every step we hope and pray a cure is on the way.

In December, 2008, Shirley and I took a cruise down the Danube River. After Shirley spent two years receiving chemo and radiation treatments, this was her reward. We went with church friends from Olive Branch and Our Saviour's. We started our journey in Nuremberg and ended it in Vienna. Along the way we stopped at Kris Kringle Christmas Markets in several towns. Nuremberg's market is famous for the Beautiful Fountain and the glockenspiel. Our Lady's Church forms a beautiful backdrop.

WINGS OF FAITH

Wooden hand carved Christmas ornaments are among the most popular items for sale. The market, with its' red and white striped booths, attracts more than a million tourists each year. Among the many delicious items to eat is their Lebkuchen. It is a spiced, glazed gingerbread that goes very well with Gluhwein, a warm mulled wine that is sold in souvenir mugs. Travelling by ship rather than by bus is wonderful. The food is delicious and everyone's dietary needs are met. While having breakfast, our bed was converted into a couch and our cabin was thoroughly cleaned. After dinner, we gathered for karaoke or other entertainment. Our couch was converted back into our bed with fresh, clean sheets. Our cabin had a balcony allowing us to sit outside. We fed the swans in the river below and enjoyed the beautiful views. At night, we could sit and gaze at the stars above. Along the shore, mistletoe seemed to be in every tree and orchards of apricot trees were everywhere. We travelled by night and docked at Regensburg one morning. It is a gothic city dominated by many cathedrals. We entered the city through a gate that was once a Roman fortification. Most of the Kris Kringle markets are located within walking distance of the Danube River. There were also Christmas services held at noon in several cathedrals. As we sailed toward our next destination, Passau, we passed the famous monument, Valhalla.

The city of Passau is located at the mouth of three rivers, the Danube, the Inn, and the Ilz. The city got its' name from a Roman fort. With three rivers merging at one place, flooding is commonplace. You can see water lines on buildings, some six to eight feet high. Their Kris Kringle market was very colorful but somewhat smaller than other ones. We added another Gluhwein souvenir mug to our collection. They are dated each year and have become collectibles in various shapes such as boots.

171

Salzburg is one of the most beautiful cities in the world. The Sound of Music was filmed there in 1965 and there are tours to visit the locations where the movie was filmed. We arrived on a cold, rainy day that turned into sleet later in the afternoon. Salzburg is divided into four squares; the largest being the Residenzplatz which has its' own Glockenspiel. Mozart Square is a "must see", especially his birthplace, and souvenirs abound. The majestic Hohensalzburg Fortress is near St. Peter's Church. The cemetery is considered the most beautiful and artistic in the world. The entrance is difficult to find because it is a very small gate at the back of the church. I spent a great deal of time there and was inspired to write the following poem.

MIDNIGHT AT ST. PETER'S
(Christmas Eve)

There is in the land of Mozart since the third century,
A cemetery at St. Peter's that tourists come to see.
Relatives maintain each grave site with diligence and care
Proud of the mini gardens they have created there.
On Christmas Eve in Austria, graves often fill with snow
But loved ones gather at St. Peter's as they did years ago.
They process to family grave sites with a candle in their hand
On this holist of nights here in this ancient land.
From one candle, all are lighted – soon thousands are aglow
And the gardens of St. Peter's seem to blossom in the snow!
The sound of music warms their hearts as they sing, "Silent Night"
At midnight in the gardens while all is calm and bright.

WINGS OF FAITH

The Mirabell Garden fountain was frozen solid that day. This was the scene of the children playing on the steps and riding their bicycles in the movie. Upon returning to our ship, the Aria in the evening, the metal gangplank was completely iced over causing Shirley to slip and fall. Her arthritic knee began to swell immediately and she was in pain for days. As a result of the fall, she was unable to leave the ship the following day to visit the Melk Abbey and Vienna. Shirley insisted that I go ahead with the group.

Our last day of the trip was spent in the Austrian capital, home of the Habsburg family. History oozes from the pores of this city. Everything seems larger than life from the Schonbrunn Palace to the Rathaus "Town Hall" and the luxurious State Opera House. You feel like you are on a movie set among these historical scenes. The Kris Kringle Market was located across from the Town Hall. During the rest of the year that space becomes a concert area for people like Andre Rieu.

We were there in the evening with all the beautiful Christmas lights making it a magical place to visit. I got another Gluhwein mug to add to our collection and a beautiful red poinsettia lace centerpiece which sits on our dining room table every December. What beautiful memories these mugs and the centerpiece are to remind us of our European Christmas cruise. Travel is wonderful, but it still confirms the old saying, "There's no place like home."

173

WINGS OF FAITH

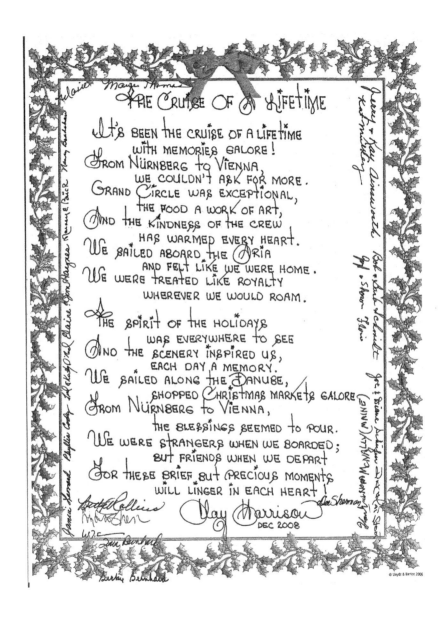

WINGS OF FAITH

Once Shirley completed two years of chemo and radiation treatments, we began participating in the annual Williamsburg Relay For Life, she the survivor and me, the caregiver. The CWF provides a luminary for every cancer survivor in our congregation. Sadly, each year we gain some and lose some. Every year I write a poem of hope about cancer which is read by our friend and Relay coordinator, Charlotte Pope.

RAYS OF HOPE
For Relay for Life 2017

Because there's hope, we fight the fight and walk the extra mile.
With hope a cure will soon be found, we walk it with a smile.
Our load is heavy, tears may fall, but still we carry on
Remembering those who came before, and those who now are gone.
Because there's hope, we keep the faith that comes from answered prayer
Because miracles still happen – there are angels everywhere!
We are in this fight together – no one walks alone.
Even in our darkest hour, rays of hope lead us on.
There are mountains we must climb yet, but there are valleys too,
And together we can make it and have a dream come true.
There are blessings to be counted after every trial.
Because there's hope, we fight the fight and walk the extra mile!

You say you don't believe in miracles? Surely this story will warm your heart. We came to know Erica, a police officer's wife, who was diagnosed with an aggressive type of breast cancer when she was 12 weeks pregnant with her second child. It was life threatening and she was advised to terminate

175

the pregnancy in order to save her own life. This is Erica's story, in her own words. All I can add is praise the Lord!

Erica's Story

In April of 2003, I was diagnosed with breast cancer. I was 29 years old, happily married, the mother of a 14 month old son and 12 weeks pregnant with my second child. Needless to say, this came as quite a shock to me. I knew very little about breast cancer and had no family history.

A lump was detected by my obstetrician at my first prenatal appointment. From there I was sent for a sonogram and then a mammogram which highlighted two additional areas of suspicion. After a biopsy of all three areas, my world was turned upside down. I was given less than two years to live if I did not receive the treatment I needed immediately and was told that I should consider terminating my pregnancy in order to save my life. I was devastated! I was not only faced with decisions to make about my life but about the life of my unborn child as well.

So due to my age, the fact that my cancer was determined to be extremely aggressive and the biopsy showed no clean margins, I underwent a mastectomy the following week. After several hours of surgery, my obstetrician could not locate a heartbeat, but a sonogram later showed that my unborn child was still alive.

I then needed to begin chemotherapy treatment as soon as possible. I was told that my unborn child would probably not survive chemotherapy and once again, I was faced with the decision of whether or not to go ahead and terminate my pregnancy. However, less than a month later, after receiving a second and third opinion, I began a series of five rounds of intense chemotherapy along with yet another surgery to have a mediport catheter placed in my chest for easier administration.

Through it all, I chose to fight, not only for my life, but for the life of my unborn child and on October 20, 2003, I delivered the most beautiful and healthy baby girl. It was absolutely the best day of my life to finally see her and hold her in my arms. I then had to endure nine more rounds of chemotherapy and six and a half weeks of exhausting radiation, but I am proud to say that I have now been cancer free since November of 2003, and I feel great!

I truly believe my daughter saved my life. If I would not have been pregnant, it is uncertain as to when my cancer would have been detected. I chose to name her Mia Grace which means "my gift from God." She is a miracle to me and she would be the first to tell you she is "mommy's angel." I am extremely grateful for my team of doctors and the tremendous support I received from my husband, family, friends, and co-workers. My daughter and I would not be where we are today without each and every one of them.

WINGS OF FAITH

CHAPTER SEVEN

MIA GRACE: "MY GIFT FROM GOD"

Mia's journey was a hard one from Heaven to this earth
And all who come to know her marvel at her birth.
For her mother had a cancer when she was conceived
And there were no easy answers except that Mom believed.
Erica's father was a pastor who shaped her tender years
And her faith in God is stronger than all her doubts and fears.
Through prayers and supplication, she won the victory
For Mia Grace is healthy and Mom is cancer free!
Some say there are no miracles but they don't love and know
A gift from God named Mia Grace who sets our hearts aglow!

In April, 2017, I joined the survivor list when I had a 2 1/2 hour skin cancer surgery on my face. My plastic surgeon, Jonstuart Guarnieri, put in about 100 stitches and I have no scar. We never know what the future holds, but we do know who holds the future! In December 2017, I had a second 2 1/2 hour skin cancer surgery on my forehead. Again, Dr. Guarnieri did a masterful job. I am still Shirley's caregiver and she has always been mine, especially when I underwent quad bypass surgery. We try to live life to the fullest every day and praise God for the blessings that come our way.

I have often wondered where one goes for solace and comfort in times of tribulation when they have no spiritual guidance. How do they cope who have no hope? Everyone needs a way to cope with stress. For me, worship at a Bible based, faith sharing church, and daily devotions is my way to cope. Each morning, I thank God for the new day and pray for strength to

WINGS OF FAITH

do what He wants me to do. Sometimes at night, I fall asleep while I am praying.

Poetry has been my way of coping and capturing daily events by painting word pictures that praise God and offer hope. A newspaper article once described me as "THE POET OF HOPE."

In April of 2007 everyone in America became a Virginia Tech fan after 32 students and teachers were slain. As usual, the politicians and the NRA did nothing. On April 19, 2007, I was helping Shirley at Our Saviour's when they tolled the church bells at noon in memoriam for those who were slain. I wrote a poem, (I Know For Whom the Bell Tolls" while they were tolling.

Too many times has this scenario repeated itself and those in power do nothing to enact sensible gun laws. Our founders must be turning over in their graves!

I KNOW FOR WHOM THE BELL TOLLS

I know for whom the bell tolls this lovely April day.
It tolls for Virginia Tech and those who passed away.
It tolls for those who died too soon before their song was sung,
For the freshmen and the seniors, the innocent and young.
It tolls too for the faculty who perished on that day
When evil stalked the hallways and snatched their lives away.
It tolls for those who mourn today the wounded and the dead
With broken hearts and tear dimmed eyes, flags half-staff overhead.
It tolls for friends and family and those we never knew
Who left behind fond memories and dreams that won't come true.
It tolls for all whose lives were changed in such an awful way.
I know for whom the bell tolls this lovely April day.

WINGS OF FAITH

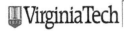

Charles W. Steger, President
210 Burruss Hall (0131)
Blacksburg, Virginia 24061
540/231-6231 Fax: 540/231-4265
E-mail: president@vt.edu
www.vt.edu   www.president.vt.edu

August 1, 2008

Dear Mr. Harrison:

Although it has been nearly a year since we received a kind note from your friend, Irma Boggs Gustafson, along with the touching poem you wrote, entitled I Know for Whom the Bell Tolls, expressing sympathy and understanding following the tragedy that befell Virginia Tech last spring, please know that we are deeply grateful for your care and concern.

We have gone through many dark days, yet we continue to find comfort in the outpouring of thoughtfulness and compassion from people such as yourself and Mrs. Gustafson. We are continuing to heal and striving to honor those we lost by making every day count.

Please continue to keep the Virginia Tech family in your thoughts and prayers and, again, thank you for your kindness and support..

Sincerely,

Charles W. Steger
President

CWS/dal

Invent the Future

VIRGINIA POLYTECHNIC INSTITUTE AND STATE UNIVERSITY
An equal opportunity, affirmative action institution

WINGS OF FAITH

WHERE DO NONBELIEVERS GO?

Where do nonbelievers go in times of deep distress?
Where do they go for comfort when they are under stress?
How can they be forgiven when they do not forgive?
Where do nonbelievers go when they lose their will to live?
How do they cope with sorrows that tear their world apart?
Where do they find an anodyne to mend a broken heart?
Where do they find a miracle when they are all alone
And they have no one to pray to when they ache to the bone?
Where do nonbelievers go who say there is no God,
When their hearts are heavy laden with a rocky road to trod?
Where do they go who have no faith in things they cannot see?
Where do nonbelievers go to end their misery?

FERGUSON

Protestors marched from coast to coast to express their point of view...
Shouts of "Hands up; don't shoot!" made us wonder what was true.
From dark streets across America into every living room,
Our nation's conscience was on trial...there was nothing to assume.
The pundits had a lot to say, the social critics too.
In the court of public opinion, each day brought something new.
Festering wounds had been reopened from Selma and Jim Crow.
The hope that has been Martin's dream still has miles to go.
When the violence is over, all blood looks the same.
Let the evidence determine where to place the blame.
Let us peacefully assemble, walk together hand in hand
And pray God soon will lead us to Martin's dreamed-of-land.

181

WINGS OF FAITH

After the tragic church massacre at Mother Emanuel in Charleston, S.C., a city-wide memorial service was held at First Baptist Church in Williamsburg. It is an historic church where the Freedom Bell is housed.

In honor of the nine families of the slain parishioners, a notebook of condolences was compiled for each family. My poem, A Time To Mourn, was included in each notebook.

When President Obama sang Amazing Grace at the memorial service in Charleston, the nation saw what a "consoler-in-chief" should be. It was an historic moment.

A TIME TO MOURN

Innocent blood has been spilled at "Mother Emanuel,"
An AME church in Charleston that history knows well.
Racism reared its ugly head and left nine people dead,
Nine Bibles fallen to the floor with bloodstains turning red.
Hearts and souls have been broken – this is a time to mourn.
Countless prayers are being spoken for the grief we have borne.
The killer is in custody, no remorse on his face,
And yet he has been forgiven with dignity and grace.
Hate has lost another battle – nine saints have gone above.
God has wrapped his arms around them and welcomed them with love.
An evil has been overcome – a healing has begun.
As we grow in faith together, God bless us everyone!

WINGS OF FAITH

Perhaps the saddest day of my lifetime occurred on December 14, 2012, when twenty beautiful children were slain eleven days before Christmas and Congress did nothing in the aftermath. Once again, politicians sold their souls to the NRA.

"Suffer little children, and forbid them not to come unto me, for of such is the kingdom of heaven." Matthew 19:14 NIV. Who was protecting the children then, or on Valentine's Day six years later in Parkland, Florida? When will those who have the power to change things put politics aside and enact common sense gun laws? Perhaps today's students will be tomorrow's voters who will make a difference. Mass shootings with weapons of war are all too common now. Wake up, America!

SANDY HOOK

It was a day like many others with Christmas on the way
And happy children looking forward to a joyous holiday.
They had no way of knowing there'd be no joy today
For an evil darker than night was heading their way.
Shots rang out at Sandy Hook and lives were changed that day
As the slaughter of innocents stole twenty lives away.
The intruder showed no mercy and there was hell to pay
For six heroic teachers who dared to block his way!
The carnage was unimaginable at Sandy hook that day!
If our Founding Fathers were alive, whatever would they say?
Fewer lives would have been lost and some would be alive today
If our national politics didn't stand in the way.

183

CHAPTER SEVEN

TO LOSE A CHILD AT CHRISTMASTIME

To lose a child at Christmastime is utter agony.
Shattered dreams fill broken lives with pain and misery,
Unwrapped presents beneath Christmas trees, silent, empty rooms...
Twenty lives nipped in the bud before they got to bloom.
Decorations lose their luster when hearts begin to break,
When lips begin to tremble and hands begin to shake.
To lose a child hurts anytime, but the pain is magnified
When tragedy strikes at Christmastime and tears you up inside.
Children are precious gifts from God; they fill our lives with love,
Every one a tiny angel when they are called above.
However brief their journey here, our hearts are fuller grown
For having known and loved them...they're missed now that they're gone!

For several years, eight members of Olive Branch formed a support group called "Spike and the Gang." Our leader, Donna, spikes her hair, thus she was Spike. Dot, Lois, David, Gertie, Nancy, Shirley, and I were known as "the gang." We even had tee shirts made. When we walked into a restaurant, people stared at us as if we were going to sing for them!

We went out to eat, a lot, went to plays, had our annual Christmas parties at Nancy's house (because she has more Santa things than the real Mrs. Claus,) and we took bus trips together from Vermont to Niagara Falls and Ottawa, "the land of duty free!"

Due to cancer, Lois had one leg amputated and I was her "designated wheelchair driver." She hopped down the bus steps one at a time into my arms, got in her chair, and off we went. Getting back on the bus was more difficult. I was well paid with lots of hugs!

Dot suffered kidney failure and we took her to dialysis treatments until she had enough, decided to stop the treatments, and let nature take its course. Within a short time, both Dot and Lois occupied the same bed in the same room at our Hospice House.

During the last months of her life, Lois received food, visits, cards, and phone calls from the CWF (Christian Women's Fellowship) ladies of Olive Branch at least twice a week. Shirley organized a schedule to insure that Lois was kept in good spirits once the diagnosis was terminal. Shirley was with her when Dr. Ellis had to give her the bad news. It helps to have a friend who will cry with you in times like these.

Before Lois passed away, she was honored by the CWF as Daughter of God at their annual luncheon. There wasn't a dry eye in the room.

WINGS OF FAITH

Daughter of God

Her smile is like Spring sunshine
when roses are in bloom,
Her hugs are warm as candlelight
when she enters a room.
Her Faith is so much stronger
than all her doubts and fears,
And her bouquets of blessings
are watered with her tears.
Her eyes have seen some hard times
fall like summer rain,
But through all the disappointments,
her joy outweighs the pain!
Her friends are like the stars above
on a cloudless night
For she exudes the Christian love
that keeps our spirits bright.
She continues to inspire us
in new and loving ways
And her courage and her kindness
are worthy of our praise.
We admire her and we love her
for love has been her shield,
And today we're proud to honor
our friend, Lois Beddingfield!

The CWF and Clay Harrison

May 9, 2009

WINGS OF FAITH

CHAPTER SEVEN

H-E-A-R-T, Inc.

Police officers and their families sometimes become crime victims too. A Williamsburg police officer came home after working a midnight shift, went to bed, and fell fast asleep. His wife went out back to take out the trash. A stranger saw her, attacked her, dragged her into the woods behind her house, and raped her in broad daylight at knifepoint. She feared for her life with her husband sleeping only a short distance away. The suspect spared her life and ran away but her life was changed forever. She was a Christian, but the horrific experience left her paranoid. She was afraid to leave her house alone. In time, she began to heal by singing and telling her story in churches. She also became an advocate for DNA testing in Virginia. She founded a support group called H-E-A-R-T, Inc. She spoke at our church in 2004 and I wrote a poem and song for her.

September 16, 2004

Dear Clay,

What a wonderful surprise to find in my mailbox! Thank you for the beautiful poem and songs. They are such a sweet and thoughtful gift. I can hardly wait to have my friend help me with the songs on her piano. Your words of encouragement will remain in my heart and will be used to help encourage others. May God bless you and your wife.

Sincerely,
Debbie Smith
H-E-A-R-T, Inc.

Virginia also made national headlines before we moved here. There were a series of unsolved rapes and murders along the beautiful Colonial Parkway which is famous for the wild onions that grow there on the bank of the York River. There are no street lights and it became a lover's lane at night, which is never a good idea. There have been many theories about the unsolved murders after such a long time, including one that the suspect was a police officer or a security guard. Sadly, the rapist and murderer continues to evade capture.

SOMEONE MAY BE WATCHING

Someone may be watching you with evil on their mind
To turn your world upside down and leave it far behind.
In one unguarded moment, you find you're not alone
And the peaceful life you cherished will be forever gone.
The rapist will terrorize you until he's had his way,
And you'll be changed forevermore after that dreadful day.
You'll find it hard to sleep at night without seeing his face,
And he may be someone you know who's fallen in disgrace.
Perhaps you may want to die but that is not the way,
Our loving God will give you strength as you cope day by day.
With faith in God, and therapy, you can survive it all –
Beware, someone may be watching who would like to see you fall!

WINGS OF FAITH

CHAPTER SEVEN

Washington, D.C.

City of monuments and memories,
historical streets lined with cherry trees...
Seat of government and builder of dreams,
city of parks and four sporting teams.
City of hope and American pride,
tomb of the Unknowns who valiantly died...
The National Mall so grandly displayed,
echoes of Freedom and great speeches made.
City of commerce, opportunity for all,
a fortress of faith and a tear stained Wall...
A White House built for its leaders to live,
a city with heart that's willing to give.
Maker of laws beneath a Capitol dome,
thrills of a lifetime for all to take home...
A National Cathedral so noble to see,
proud beacon of faith in the land of the free.
A Center for Arts, a National Zoo,
a Smithsonian filled with things old and new...
A city of hope in moments like these,
city of monuments and memories!

One of the scourges of our society is human trafficking. I can't imagine a more dehumanizing crime. Those who survive these horrors will have physical and emotional scars forever. The nightmares never end.

189

WINGS OF FAITH

There is a home in Williamsburg for women who have been rescued and are assisted in being rehabilitated back into society. They need food, clothing, lots of tender loving care, and a job, a sense of self worth. The CWF ladies of Olive Branch have offered such help.

The I-95 corridor is notorious for these victims being transported up and down the east coast. It pays to be observant if you see suspicious activities at rest stops. Get tag numbers and alert the police. You could be someone's hero and save their life.

STOLEN LIVES

Christians, we have a problem here in the U.S.A.,
For lives are being stolen in cities every day!
The chains of modern slavery are stretching far and wide
And global trade in human flesh is a crime we can't abide.
Women and children are being sold at an alarming rate
For sexual exploitation and forced labor in our state!
The victims are dehumanized in ways we cannot know
While profits from their suffering multiply and grow.
It's a universal problem that's landed on our shores
And we must work to break the chains of slavery evermore.
The wounds are deep and hard to heal but we can do our part
To bind their wounds and offer hope to every broken heart.

Kayla's Story

In 2014, an American aid worker, Kayla Mueller, from Prescott, Arizona, was killed during a bombing raid on an ISIS stronghold in Syria. Kayla was held captive by an ISIS leader who forced her to marry him. Before she was captured, she stated in an

WINGS OF FAITH

interview, "Peace is not something you wish for, it is something you make."

I have heard that John Lennon uttered those words also before his untimely death. I am certain that Kayla lived those words all the days of her life. I was inspired to write the poem, Peace, and entered it in a contest in the Daily Press Annual Reader's Choice contest. I told Kayla's story all around town during the voting time. I lost by one vote in the last second. I wanted her story to be told and that was achieved. It was printed in the paper. I was able to locate her parents and send them the poem.

The Kayla Mueller Family

Dear Clay,   June 2015

We want to thank you for your profoundly apropos poem, "Peace," which you created as a tribute to our daughter Kayla. Each verse inspires a mental image of our beloved daughter's faithfully living as an ambassador of peace everywhere she went....even when held captive.

In the Sermon on the Mount, Jesus told the faithful, "You are the light of the world....let your light shine before men, that they may see your good deeds and praise your Father in heaven." (Matt 5: 14, 16) Your beautiful poem, "Peace," will serve to magnify Kayla's bright and far ranging light, all to the glory of God.

Our family will always cherish your most meaningful gift created in honor of Kayla.

May God continue to bless you and yours.

Gratefully,

Marsha Carl

Marsha and Carl

WINGS OF FAITH

PEACE

"Peace is not something you wish for, it is something you make."
Kayla Mueller: ISIS hostage killed in Syria

Peace is not something you wish for, it is something you make.
It's a dream you keep on dreaming even when you're awake.
Peace is the way you treat others regardless of race.
It's a simple act of kindness, a smile on your face.
Peace reaches across borders, welcomes strangers next door.
It gives hope to the homeless who arrive on our shore.
Peace is the silver lining behind the darkest cloud.
It's the calm voice of reason that quiets angry crowds.
Peace is love put into action when faith leads the way;
It's compassion in its purest form for those we meet each day.
It's sharing our resources giving more than we take.
Peace is not something you wish for, it is something you make.

WINGS OF FAITH

CHAPTER SEVEN

Violence can rear its ugly face when you least expect it. On April 22, 2016, a father whose wife was pregnant with their second child went to the local Farm Fresh to buy a box of donuts early on a Sunday morning. A mentally ill man from another city shot him to death for no apparent reason. He would later say that God told him to do it.

On Sunday, May 1, a prayer service for healing and support was held at Our Saviour's Lutheran Church for the Ryan Maness family. Seven local pastors presided and I had the honor of writing a poem for the program, "Tragedy At Farm Fresh."

TRAGEDY AT FARM FRESH

There are tragedies so shocking they bring us all to tears
Because we thought that in our town "it could not happen here!"
Who would think on Sunday morning a stranger would appear
And kill someone he did not know, someone we held so dear.
Aisle six became a crime scene at our local Farm Fresh store.
All who were there shall not forget the bloodstains on the floor.
There are things we don't understand known only unto God.
We may never know the reasons here on this earthly sod.
Our God's love abides within us – He knows the pain we feel,
And through prayerful supplication we can begin to heal.
This is a time for mourning – in time it too will pass
For by God's grace we can survive and peace will come at last!

193

Our son's first marriage ended in divorce after ten years. Waiting in the wings was his true love, Joy, who really is a joy to know! She was raised in the Philippines. Her parents, George and Virginia, are wonderful people. George is one month younger than I am. He served in the military as I did and while here for Joy's wedding, he had heart bypass surgery as I did.

The Aquino's are loving, generous people. They brought gifts for everyone who attended the wedding – approximately 100 adults and 40 children. The ceremony was performed jointly by a priest, as Joy is Catholic, and Mark's favorite Methodist pastor from Tampa, Bill Corristan.

Mark was so overwhelmed with joy, no pun intended, that he cried while repeating his vows and everyone needed a tissue. The reception was a gala affair. Joy's brother, Paul, put together a collage of photos showing Mark and Joy growing up from their childhood to adulthood in two different countries. The similarities were absolutely amazing! The newlyweds surprised everyone with an upbeat dance they had secretly been practicing and followed that with the traditional dance with the bride's parents.

WINGS OF FAITH

Joy's father was experiencing heart problems and needed bypass surgery which he preferred to have done while he was here in the states. The surgery went very well and he and Virginia were able to spend more time with Joy and Mark while he completed rehab before returning home to the Philippines.

For their belated honeymoon, Mark and Joy travelled to the Philippines. Joy's parents met them at the Manila airport and drove them to their hotel. As luck would have it, there was a typhoon headed for Manila and no one could leave the hotel. No other rooms were available so George and Virginia ended up spending the night with the newlyweds in the honeymoon suite! Mark shared a bed with new father-in-law while Joy slept with her mother. Family is everything!

"All's well that ends well" it has often been said. Following the cleanup, Mark and Joy had a great time going sightseeing with Joy's parents. Mark fell in love with Philippine food, especially some of the tropical fruits that grow there. He experienced his first Philippine Buko Pie made fresh daily from coconuts and sold by street vendors. He said they were heavenly but he couldn't figure out how to get one through Customs! The highlight of their trip was a visit to the Ark Avilon Zoo where Mark was able to hold and pet exotic animals which was a thrill for him as he has always been a major animal lover.

George and Virginia returned for Bella's first birthday. It was a mega party complete with a clown and a magic show. Many friends of Joy's family from the area were there along with their children. The party was held at a recreation center and the kids had fun on the playground. Bella had a ball with all the attention and it was a real pleasure for us to be able to visit with George and Virginia again.

WINGS OF FAITH

LITTLE ANGEL
(for Bella - August 15, 2013)

Little angel sent from heaven, you came a long, long way
To bless us with your presence here on earth today.
Little angel, sweet and precious how beautiful you are!
The sparkle in your tiny eyes outshines the brightest star.
Little angel soft and cuddly, we're so glad you came.
Your daddy, Mark, and mommy, Joy, will never be the same!
There are many who will love you as you grow in grace,
And they'll know you're an angel when they see your sweet face.
Today will always be your birthday as the years pass by,
And the wondrous things you'll see will keep you asking, "Why?"
Little angel how we love you and pray you'll love us too.
May God shower you with blessings and make your dreams come true!

WINGS OF FAITH

CHAPTER 8

FAITH IN ACTION

"For we walk by faith, not by sight." II Corinthians 5:7 NIV

OLIVE BRANCH CHRISTIAN CHURCH
(Disciples of Christ)

In an Emily Dickinson poem she states, "I'm nobody. Are you nobody too!" Certainly the Belle of Amhurst was not a nobody. Neither are we, my friends. We are created in His image and therefore heirs to His kingdom. Jesus said, "The kingdom of God is within you." Wow! We may never be rich or famous, but as faithful servants, great is our reward in heaven!

WINGS OF FAITH

I have been a face in the crowd, the barefoot boy looking at things I could never possess. I know how hurtful that can be when you have no money to buy your mother a Christmas present. If only we could eliminate GREED from the world. No one would go to bed hungry or be homeless. Everyone could have an education and decent health care. We have lived in the world of "Let them eat cake" for far too long!

I admire the wealthy like Oprah Winfrey, who uses her power and influence to make the world a better place for those less fortunate. It is sad to see how often our idols squander their fortunes on self indulgence and die penniless having helped no one. The exception of course is Warren Buffet. Imagine how different the world would be if all the billionaires in the world were as generous with their money as he is!

I have often stated that God has a plan for your life. He also gives us free will to accept or deny Him. There's a famous painting of Jesus standing at a door and knocking. The door has no doorknob. The person inside must open the door and let Him in. I invited Christ into my life at age sixteen. Some people, like the thief on the cross next to Jesus, don't invite Him in until it's almost too late.

When we choose to walk in His footsteps, He guides us on our spiritual journey by sending angels, seen and unseen, to light the path before us. I would like to introduce you to some "angels" who have impacted my life. I'm sure you know some as well wherever you are on your spiritual journey.

There should be a picture of Ronnie and Elaine under the word FRIENDSHIP in Webster's dictionary. When we moved to Williamsburg, we didn't know anyone here. The first winter brought a five inch snowstorm. It was beautiful, but we couldn't

WINGS OF FAITH

back out of our driveway. Coming from Florida, we had never needed a snow shovel or snow boots. Everyone had assured us that it "rarely snows here." Before we moved in, there was an ice storm that left our neighborhood without power for almost a week!

I was shoveling snow with my garden shovel when Ronnie and Elaine arrived with snow shovels and a birthday cake. They had heard it was my birthday. With the proper equipment, my driveway was cleared in a hurry due to the kindness of people who barely knew us.

When hurricane Isabel hit our area in 2003, a tree fell across our driveway and we were stuck again. As if they had ESP, Ronnie and Elaine appeared once more, this time with a chain saw. They helped me and my neighbors, who needed help as well. Elaine took our frozen food to store in her extra freezer. They had generator power!

Ronnie had a passion for beekeeping and was named "Beekeeper of the Year." He allowed me to help him harvest the honey from time to time.

WINGS OF FAITH

CHAPTER EIGHT

AFTERMATH

"Prayer can't stop a hurricane," I heard someone say,
"Even the prayers of godly men won't chase the storm away."
Perhaps that's true but I believe that God protects His own,
And through the darkest, wind-blown night, we know we're not alone.
Trees may fall and shingles fly but somehow we survive,
And once the storm is over we're thankful we're alive!
Our losses may be many when all is said and done,
But our blessings too are many when counted one by one.
Whatever losses we sustained, others lost much more.
Some lost everything they had on the mid-Atlantic shore.
We licked our wounds, praised the Lord and started helping others,
And somewhere in the aftermath strangers became brothers!
Prayer may not stop a hurricane or chase the storm away,
But prayer became the anchor that's holding fast today.

Random acts of kindness are routine for these earthly angels. Sadly, we lost Ronnie to a massive heart attack on December 28, 2013. Elaine provided ministry to the elderly at her respite house, Interlude, for ten years. We have been blessed to have them in our lives. Elaine never forgets a birthday or anniversary. She continues to teach monthly Bible studies at Interlude, sing in the choir, and serve as an elder at Olive Branch.

Our friends, Bob and Judy, rescue animals and call their property Rascals Run. For more than two decades, they have cared for horses, donkeys, and many dogs and cats. When they needed someone to help out so they could take a vacation, Shirley and I volunteered to feed their animals and give them lots of TLC.

WINGS OF FAITH

Bob fought a long, courageous battle with cancer and passed away in April, 2012. During that time, I fed the animals twice a day, cleaned the barn, and scooped poop so Judy could give her undivided attention to Bob. When he passed away, I wrote a poem called, "The King Of Rascals Run."

Judy has downsized now and we all agree that by now Bob has built a big red barn somewhere in heaven! Judy continues to sing in our choir and has served as an elder.

When Bob was property chair at Olive Branch, I helped him plant a row of Encore azaleas on one side of the church. While on our knees planting, Bob stated, "Long after we're gone, these flowers will lend their beauty to our church." How true, Bob, how true!

WINGS OF FAITH

CHAPTER EIGHT

THE KING OF RASCALS RUN

Bob was the King of Rascals Run, a kind, generous man
Who rescued abused, unwanted pets with Judy hand-in-hand.
Bob loved and cared for more animals than Noah in his ark,
And turned a few green acres into a nature park.
Bob was a man who loved the Lord with all his heart and soul
And he gladly served as an elder to make the broken whole.
Love and kindness defined the man all throughout his life,
And no husband was more devoted to caring for his wife.
Perhaps God took Bob to Heaven to spare him further pain.
Although our hearts are aching, our loss is Heaven's gain!
Rascals Run won't be the same now without his footsteps there,
But we're richer for having known him and his tender, loving care!

CEMETERY

Between the headstones jonquils grow when spring is in the air.
They spring to life among the dead that loved ones buried there.
They seem to say, "Remember us who lived here long ago.
We are not dead; we've risen too where Heaven's gardens grow."

Two of our favorite people at Olive Branch are Steve and Donna. Donna is a retired school teacher and also a cancer survivor with a powerful testimony. She and some of her card-making ladies get together and make hand crafted greeting cards for the Sunday school class to send to members who are sick or have a special occasion. She also teaches card

WINGS OF FAITH

making and Shirley is one of her students. They each make hundreds of cards every year. It is a true ministry of love. I even get to add a verse now and then.

Donna's husband, Steve, is a blacksmith and a talented painter as well. He can work magic with a piece of steel or a paint brush. We have one of Steve's crosses on the apex of our storage shed in our back yard. From my chair in the living room, I look through sliding glass doors and see his cross framed by my cherry blossoms on Easter morning.

Steve's ornate flag holder, which he made for Shirley while she was undergoing chemotherapy, greets everyone approaching our front door. He also makes spikes like those used to nail Jesus to the cross. I use them as props for some of my poetry readings. They are both very generous with their time and talents.

Our very dear friend Naomi lost her battle with cancer in 2016. She was a lovely English lass with the voice of an angel. She founded Backstage Productions in 1997 to give children of all ages a chance to act, sing and dance. They perform five or six plays a year, free of charge, at churches and libraries, and

WINGS OF FAITH

even at Walt Disney World. Every other year, they perform "A Christmas Carol." During the intermission, Naomi would sing "O, Holy Night" with heartfelt passion.

Her cancer was diagnosed during Lent in 2015 and she was given a short time to live. Her prayer was that God would grant her one more Christmas with her family. When we celebrated Christmas in July at Olive Branch that year, packing shoeboxes filled with toys for the Samaritan's Purse Project, Naomi sang "O, Holy Night" with tear-filled eyes. Needless to say, there wasn't a dry eye in the sanctuary.

Naomi's prayer was answered. She spent Christmas with us, and it would be the last one. Her cancer returned with a vengeance before Easter in 2016. Even a day long, five surgeon procedure at Johns Hopkins could not save her. She passed away that October, but Backstage Productions continues under the direction of her daughter, Colleen.

Naomi and I were very close. I would sit on her couch and read poetry to her for an hour. Shirley and I would take her to lunch most Fridays when she felt up to it. While she was getting her chemo treatments, I read to her the entire three hours. It calmed her and she had no fear whatsoever. Christmas, rodeos, and blue butterflies were some of her favorite things. I planted a blue butterfly bush by her grave in our church cemetery. We decorated it with miniature lights one Christmas and blue butterflies the next.

WINGS OF FAITH

NAOMI: A FOND REMEMBRANCE

It's been a year since you left us for your new home Above.
We miss the beauty of your smile, and your heartwarming love.
We'd love to hear you sing once more about that "Holy Night"
And celebrate Christ's birthday in church by candlelight.
There's so much we'd like to tell you, so much we'd like to know
About your new home in Heaven where crystal rivers flow.
You left us with fond memories – we treasure every one.
You inspired us with your courage until your race was run.
Your life was such a blessing to all who came your way.
You spoke with the voice of an angel each time we heard you pray.
Each time we see blue butterflies, feel the sun's warm embrace,
We sense your presence with us, your smile time can't erase.

On December 13, 2017, we laid to rest our oldest member, Ruby Jones, who was a young 104 1/2 years old. She lived her whole life in our community. The sanctuary was overflowing with family, friends, and memories. After I read her celebration

WINGS OF FAITH

of life poem, I remarked that, "There are two types of people gathered here today - those related to Miss Ruby, and those who wish they were."

THE MATRIACH OF CROAKER

She was the matriarch of Croaker more than a century,
A humble farmer's daughter who grew her family tree.
She was the mother of three daughters and Wesley's loving wife.
She was a jewel of great beauty all the days of her life.
When times were bad she learned to cope through fortitude and prayer.
Ruby kept the home fires burning with tender loving care.
Her Christian faith sustained her whenever there were tears.
Her blessings always multiplied to nullify her fears.
To know Ruby was to love her, her kind, unselfish ways,
She was truly heaven-sent and God extended her days.
Sweet memories remain forever bright as the stars above.
She's gone but Ruby blessed us with a legacy of love!

WINGS OF FAITH

On March 24, 2018, approximately 800,000 students, teachers, and parents held "the march for our lives" on Washington, D.C. Ironically, the president and Congress were not there. Eight hundred other marches were held from coast to coast and on every continent except Antarctica.

They came to protest gun control across the U.S.A. in honor of those who died at Marjorie Stoneman Douglas High School on Valentine's Day. It will be an uphill battle. The NRA won't give an inch, but the battle can be won in the voting booth. It's just a matter of time.

THE MARCH FOR OUR LIVES
(Washington, D.C. 3/24/2018)

They are marching by the thousands to have their voices heard
Because those who hold the power have failed to keep their word.
Politicians keep making promises they don't intend to keep
While the slain of Stoneman Douglas sleep their eternal sleep.
Our schools have lost the innocence we knew in days gone by.
We never had to worry then if we were going to die.
We never saw the weapons of war so many now embrace.
Since Columbine and Sandy Hook, they are now commonplace.
We've seen death and devastation, broken hearts that never heal,
But the NRA does not care – to them it's no big deal!
Teenage leaders of tomorrow, our proud, determined youth,
Are determined to keep on marching right to the voting booth!

WINGS OF FAITH

In 1986, Harold Warp, Sr., found one of my Salesian poems and asked for permission to use it in his company's annual Christmas book, Warp's Yuletide Greetings. There are over 30,000 dealers selling Warp's top quality plastic products in America. The books are sent to them at Christmastime.

I didn't hear from Mr. Warp, Sr., again, but his son, Harold G., contacted me in 1994, and they have used my poems every year since. The books contain holiday poems, black and white photos, and news about their products. The color cover is the courthouse dome at Warp's Pioneer Village in the "Christmas City," Minden, Nebraska, a tourist attraction founded by Harold Warp, Sr.

Shirley and I met Harold and his charming wife, Mary, while we were on a bus trip to Mackinac Island in 2010. They have a summer home above the famous Grand Hotel. They were leaving to return to Chicago but we had a nice visit before they

WINGS OF FAITH

left. After corresponding with him for seventeen years, it was a real pleasure to meet such a distinguished businessman and fellow Christian, another stepping stone on my spiritual journey.

Bob Kircher was a musician in the Big Band era, a World War II vet, and leader of the Shriner's band in Cincinnati most of his life. He passed away a few years ago and left behind a treasure trove of music. I am honored to have written lyrics for 128 of his songs. Bob found one of my lyrical poems in a Salesian book, contacted me, and asked permission to set it to music. It was the beginning of a beautiful friendship.

My old fashioned, lyrical poetry meshed well with his musical skills. Bob and his wife Marilyn belonged to the Clifton Music Club. Each year at Christmas, they performed their Winter Sing program. Most of the programs consisted of traditional Christmas music. Bob would include six or seven of our original songs including, "I'm Going Caroling with Marilyn" which I wrote for his wife. I also wrote a theme song for his band, "You'll Never Walk Alone, Child."

WINGS OF FAITH

In the winter of 2004, Bob composed a piece of music to pay tribute to all soldiers in all wars. It begins with a drum roll and ends with taps. He needed lyrics worthy of his masterpiece and asked me for help. Without hearing the music, I prayed about it. On the third day it came to me. I woke up to the oft quoted words, "Lest We Forget" running through my head. Words and music blended perfectly! Bob was amazed. It was truly divine intervention.

Our song was chosen to be performed at the World War II memorial in Washington, D.C. on April 30, 2005 to commemorate the sixtieth anniversary of the end of World War II. The Lincoln High School Band of Knights from North Carolina was chosen to perform our song with soprano, Joanna Underwood, a former student of Bob's, singing the lyrics. Bob and I met in person for the first, and only, time at the performance. He was in a wheelchair. I pushed him over to the Vietnam Memorial so he could see "the wall" while he was in town. God brings people together in mysterious ways.

Our song was performed again in public at the Williamsburg concert for Wounded Warriors by the Old Dominion Line Barbershop Quartet on November 1, 2009. It has been sung as a solo several times at Olive Branch. I've had poems set to music in Hawaii, Nashville, and Canada, but Bob and I had a special bond and I miss him.

Music is the language of the soul. It eases stress, inspires us, sets a mood, offers praise, and we can dance to it. Church music is universal. Thanks to missionaries, one can come hum the tune to "Jesus Loves Me" almost anywhere on earth, and people will recognize it.

WINGS OF FAITH

It was such a blessing working with Bob Kircher before he passed away. I play Christian CD's in my truck most of the time. If more people did this, there would be less road rage. Our highways are becoming battlefields. More people have died on America's highways than the number of soldiers who have died in World Wars!

WINGS OF FAITH

CHAPTER EIGHT

I am blessed when I attend concerts that feature patriotic and Christian music. The Bill and Gloria Gaither concerts are heartwarming, but Ray Boltz uses his music to rescue unwanted children in Kenya. He could have been a rock superstar with his talent, but he chose to create music that glorifies God. Ray's songs, "I Pledge Allegiance to the Lamb," "The Anchor Holds," "Watch the Lamb," and "Thank You," are sermons set to music.

At his concerts, Ray has a prayer book on a table in the lobby. He asks concert goers to write the names of people who need prayer in the book. Each morning Ray and his aides read the prayers requests, lay hands on the book, and pray for the names in the book. When I attended one of his concerts years ago, Ray had shaved his head to support children who were fighting cancer. Our pastor at that time, Ron Riffle, was also fighting cancer and I wrote his name in Ray's book and got him an autographed photo from Ray.

THROW AWAY CHILDREN

In the potters' fields of Kenya, life and death go hand in hand
For the children are abandoned too young to understand.
The villagers don't want them through no fault of their own,
So they're killed or abandoned by the roadside all alone.
The lucky ones are rescued but far too many die,
The tiniest of Angels who never learned to fly.
You can hear the distant drumbeats with above the lions roar
And the dying children's' heartbeats saying, "Christian, love me more!"
In the potters' fields of Kenya, hope is fading day by day
Where the tiniest of Angels are being thrown away!
WAIF, Inc.

WINGS OF FAITH

Actress Jane Russell became one of America's most famous pin-up girls after she appeared in Howard Hughes's movie, The Outlaw. Most people were unaware of her humanitarian work on behalf of homeless children. I supported her organization and received the following letter from her.

WAIF, Inc.
National Headquarters
67 Irving Place
New York, NY 10003

May 11, 1988

Dear Clay,

Thank you for your generous reponse to the needs of America's homeless children.

Through your support and goodwill, a child's life will be forever changed from one of loneliness to the love of an adopted family. Perhaps more important than anything, it's a gift that will keep on working throughout a child's life.

Thank you again for helping us make it a better year for children in need of families.

God bless,

Jane Russell
Founder

213

WINGS OF FAITH

Danny Hahlbohm
INSPIRED-ART.COM

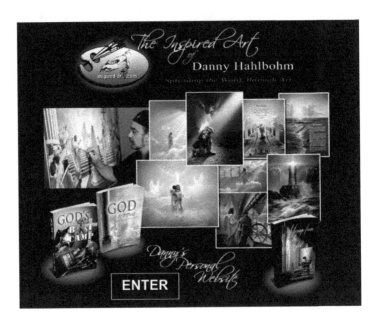

In 2014, I was contacted by renowned painter, Danny Hahlbohm, who gained worldwide acclaim with his painting, "Footprints In The Sand." Danny too found one of my poems, "Wings Of Faith," and it inspired a painting. On January 11th, Danny sent me a copy of his painting with my poem.

Subsequently, Danny used eight more of my poems on paintings already in his collection. Many of his paintings are used on Leanin' Tree greeting cards. My poems, "Wings Of Faith," and "He Who Feeds The Sparrow," are in Leanin' Tree's 2015-2016 catalog. The blessings just keep on coming!

WINGS OF FAITH

My best ideas come in the wee hours of the morning. I can't sleep until I get out of bed and write them on a legal pad. Ideas sometimes come in bunches. When I wake up in the morning, I almost don't remember writing them, as if I dreamed them into existence.

Danny sees visions in his mind before giving them life on canvas. Neither of us use our gifts for fame or fortune. It is ministry, pure and simple. I will never be a Poet Laureate writing poems few can understand, poems that never offer hope, or praise our Lord, and that's fine with me. In one of his letters, Danny stated, "I am always amazed that those who have gone through much seem to be the ones who also give much to others. Nothing seems to get God moving more than the word IMPOSSIBLE. He loves to defeat the impossible at every opportunity." Amen, Danny, Amen!

I am computer illiterate. Shirley is the computer guru at our house. When someone told me years ago they had "Googled" me and found my poems all over the Internet, I didn't know what they were talking about. Shirley checked and it was true. One of my poems had over 100,000 hits! I was truly humbled.

On November 25, 2014, at 4:52 a.m., Danny found a devotion online called, "God's Minute." The devotion that morning included my poem, "Wing's Of Faith!" I'm delighted that our paths crossed on our spiritual journeys.

215

WINGS OF FAITH

From the desk of

DANNY HAHLBOHM

inspiredart@icloud.com

January 14, 2014

Dear Clay,

Enclosed are a few sample prints I wanted to send out to you for being gracious enough
to let me use your poem "Wings Of Faith." I also submitted this image to a card company
to see if there is any interest in that as well. I will let you know if they pick that up or not.

Also I have enclosed a signed copy of my book "The God Room." I pray it will
encourage and bless you as you have blessed so many others with your talent and gift
from the Lord. It is a priveledge and honor to be working with you. May the Lord our
God receive all the glory and honor in all that we do for Him.

Keep in touch and let me know if you need anything else.

Thank you.

Sincerely,

Danny Hahlbohm

He Who Feeds the Sparrow

He who feeds the sparrow
and guides the robin's flight,
Will raise the sun tomorrow
and light the stars tonight.

His love for us is endless;
His hand can calm the sea.
He who feeds the sparrow,
still cares for you and me.

He showers us with blessings
that we might see and learn
Asking only that we listen
and love Him in return.

He who feeds the sparrow
and guides the robin's flight,
Will guide my path tomorrow
and give me peace tonight.

Clay Harrison

WINGS OF FAITH

MAY THE WINGS OF FAITH UPHOLD YOU
WHEN YOUR CROSS IS HARD TO BEAR,
AS TEMPTATIONS SURROUND YOU,
AND NO ONE SEEMS TO CARE.

MAY THE WINGS OF FAITH SURROUND YOU
AND SHIELD YOU FROM THE PAIN
WHEN SORROWS OVERCOME YOU
AND TEARDROPS FALL LIKE RAIN.

In 1979, I chanced to meet Johnny Marks and got his autograph. He signed in red ink and inscribed the musical notes to Rudolph. I loved his "Rudolph the Red Nosed Reindeer," as far back as I can remember. It was the brainchild of a relatively unknown songwriter, Johnny Marks. He saw a figure of a shiny nosed reindeer in a Montgomery Ward advertising brochure in 1939 and thought about it for a decade before Rudolph was brought to life. Reluctantly, Gene Autry was persuaded by his wife to make the recording which has sold millions of copies.

He took my address and sent me a signed photo. When he died in 1985, I wrote an article, "A Nose In The News," and it was published in the December issue of Nostalgia Scrapbook.

217

WINGS OF FAITH

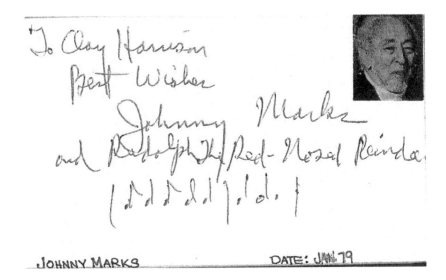

To Clay Harrison
Best Wishes
Johnny Marks
and Rudolph the Red-Nosed Reindeer

JOHNNY MARKS   DATE: JAN 79

I mentioned in my story about Janis Joplin that I worked security at many concert venues. When I wasn't outside guarding tour buses, I got to see many concerts working backstage from Elvis to the Jackson Five, from Elton John to James Brown and Ray Charles.

I have included a variety of musical autographs for this book. I especially enjoy autographs of composers who took the time to include a bar or two of musical notes from their most famous songs. I have five albums of autographed photos but can't include any of them here due to copyright issues. One on one, you get a much neater autograph than you will as part of a crowd.

WINGS OF FAITH

CHAPTER 9

IT'S A WONDERFUL LIFE

*"Now faith is the substance of things hoped for,
the evidence of things not seen." Hebrews 11:1 NIV*

"It's A Wonderful Life," is my favorite Christmas movie. I watch it at least once every year. Jimmy Stewart is my favorite actor. What you see on screen is what you get in person. I met him twice, once at a movie premiere when I lived in California, and many years later in Tampa when he was honored at Mac Dill A.F.B.

I always enjoyed the poems he read as a guest on the Tonight show. I asked him why he never published a book of his poems, better yet, a CD because his voice was so distinctive. He said

WINGS OF FAITH

he had thought about it. I gave him my current Salesian book and later received a note from him stating that he liked my poetry. From that time until his death, I sent him my books. He autographed many photos for me through the years.

Jimmy did publish his poetry book and CD. He was the most kind and humble star in the Hollywood Galaxy. When people asked for his autograph, he thanked them. He and Gloria didn't hide from people at airports. They went to the baggage claim with everyone else, with few exceptions.

In the final scenes of, "It's A Wonderful Life," the residents of Bedford Falls rally to save George Bailey from going to prison after Mr. Potter (Lionel Barrymore) stole $8,000 from his building and loan company. Among the piles of money given to George by his friends was a Bible with this note from his guardian angel: "George, no man is a failure who has friends. Thanks for the wings, Clarence."
Despite being poor most of my life, I have been rich in friends. Many friendships have been a direct result of my poetry having touched someone. God knew the gift of poetry would richly bless my life. It proves that God had a wonderful plan for my life.

WINGS OF FAITH

September 11, 1986

Dear Clay Harrison:

Thank you for your letter -- and Gloria and I are very grateful to you for your book of poems.

The book is very interesting and the way you have arranged the poems throughout the book is very impressive and we thank you again for sending it and your kind letter.

Sincerely,

James Stewart

IT'S A WONDERFUL LIFE

No one is poor who has friends even when he's penniless.
Riches come from a life well lived which brings him happiness.
He who shares his wealth with others, gives tender loving care,
Stands tall in the eyes of others whenever he is there.
He who comes in times of trouble to comfort and console,
Is blessed just for being there when sorrows take a toll.
He who stoops to life the fallen, does not blame nor condemn,
Is a friend beloved by others for they can count on him.
He who works behind the scenes helping others reach their goal,
Is someone worthy of respect for his supporting role.
He whose love is freely given in times of need or strife
Is someone God has richly blessed with a wonderful life!

WINGS OF FAITH

Some of our most enjoyable bus trips were with Educational Tours. We had a great time in Ottawa highlighted by a tour of Parliament and watching the changing of the guard. Two families related to our daughter-in-law live there and gave us evening tours not included on the bus trip.

We enjoyed visiting the Trapp Family Lodge in Stowe, Vermont. Our dear friend, Lois, was voted most inspirational passenger hopping up and down the steps off the bus into my arms. They gave her a large portrait of the lodge which she gave to me for being her designated wheelchair driver. On the return trip, we had a tour of West Point. It was most interesting walking through the cemetery where so many famous military heroes are buried.

Other special trips included Boston where we walked the Freedom Trail and visited the Old North Church where Paul Revere began his famous midnight ride. We also visited Cape Cod and Martha's Vineyard on that trip. On another trip we walked the cliffs behind the mansions at Newport, Rhode Island, and toured one of them.

We went on Christmas bus trips to the Biltmore in Asheville, N.C., Dollywood theme park in Pigeon Force, TN, and most recently the Opryland Hotel in Nashville. At each location the decorations were breathtaking!

On the bus trips, I took notes during the day, recording what we saw and did, or funny things that happened. At night in our hotel room, I composed poems which were read on the bus the next morning along with a devotional poem. When the tour was over, the travel company compiled the poems and sent them to our fellow travelers as a poetic record of the trip.

We visited the Canadian side of Niagara Falls and Toronto. While shopping and having lunch in a huge mall in Toronto, one lady in our group purchased a Woman's World magazine. She discovered one of my poems and was so excited. She was delighted to learn that I had been published in their magazine approximately forty times.

Woman's World
THE WOMAN'S WEEKLY

Heinrich Bauer North America, Inc.
270 Sylvan Avenue
Englewood Cliffs, NJ 07632
201 569 0006
fax: 201 569 3584

Hi Clay—
I'm returning only These few—
The rest are stunning, beautiful!
(So are these but not seasonal or not WW style)
So I shall keep them on file—

Thanks so much for
your lovely
careful work

Amy Chan

And we are so impressed that
an ex-police officer wrote
these touching words—
my prejudices blown away
once more!

WINGS OF FAITH

Shirley and I took several bus trips to Lancaster, PA, to see biblical productions as the Sight & Sound Theatre. In 2006, we drove to Lancaster to see a play on our own and visit a long time Salesian Missions poet, Loise Pinkerton Fritz who lives in the Lehigh Valley. We had been corresponding for many years but had never met in person.

As we were leaving Lancaster, we passed a small Amish school with a group of young children playing outside with not a care in the world. Little did we know that these children would be murdered by the local milk man within the hour. Parents of the slain children forgave the killer and reached out to console his family. The incident inspired a book, Amish Grace, which was made into a movie. Love like that is the essence of grace.

WINGS OF FAITH

CHAPTER NINE

THEY ARE WITH GOD
(In memory of the Amish children slain Oct. 2, 2006)

They are with God, the children who were slain.
They are not here to share our grief and pain.
They are with God, sheltered beneath his wings
While time stands still and choirs of angels sing.
They are with God; they left this world too soon
Like shooting stars against a rising moon.
They are with God, children we did not know,
Known only unto Him when they had to go.
They were only here for such a little while,
Now they are with God to warm Him with their smiles.
They are not dead for they shall live again!
They are with God, the children who were slain.

THE LION AND THE LAMB

Someday there will be peace on earth and wars shall be no more,
For we shall feel a rapture we've never known before.
Someday we shall see the lion lie down beside the lamb
And we shall live forevermore and worship the great I AM!

WEEP FOR THE CHILDREN
(For the children gassed in Syria, April 4, 2017)

Weep for the children who died today, those who will die tomorrow.
May their tortured faces haunt you, their suffering and sorrow.
Weep for those whose lives were stolen, those whose dreams will never be,
Dreams replaced by horrid nightmares and stark reality.

WINGS OF FAITH

I was a member of the Florida Poetry Society for forty years. We had newsletters and contests prior to the Internet but no active group meetings or poetry readings in the Tampa area while I was there. I had never met another Florida poet until Editor's Desk published my first chap book, I Am The Clay. A book signing party was held for me in Ocala. There I finally met several of the poets I had been corresponding with for many years.

Upon moving to Williamsburg, I joined the Virginia Poetry Society. Poets from different parts of the state read at our monthly meetings held at our library. Once or twice a year I get to read with the Williamsburg poets. A few years ago I did my "Mad Hatter" poetry program assisted by a lovely young girl named Rose. She would hand me the appropriate hat for each poem I read and also played Dixie on the penny whistle when I read my Johnny Reb poem. She can sing, dance, and play most instruments in the band. She has become a star in her own right and has grown too tall and become too busy

to assist me anymore. Rose is the daughter of Gigi, a well known singer and musician who once sang with Mannheim Steamroller. Her father, Dave, is part of the Old Dominion Line Barbershop Quartet. They performed my song, Lest We Forget, at the Wounded Warrior fund raiser a few years ago.

Clay reading 60's poetry

WINGS OF FAITH

 NANCY TAYLOR ROSENBERG
ABUSE OF POWER

September 10, 1997

Dear Clay:

As a former police officer myself, I know that the job can
sometimes turn hearts to stone. By your reaction to CALIFORNIA
ANGEL and the fact that you could take the time to let me know
how you enjoyed it, obviously your heart is still in tact! Your
varied background probably played some part in your appreciation
of the story, although some seemingly hardened criminals have
also written to express favorable comments.

I hope by now you have visited your local bookstore and have
introduced yourself to suspenseful reading, my latest thriller
being ABUSE OF POWER. In view of the recent news events
involving alleged abuse of authority by the New York Police
Department, it has been very well received in some circles --- to
the extent of being required reading.

Your poem "And They Say There Is No God" is simply beautiful;
nothing ostentatious and oh, so true, if only people would take
the time to look at "Magnolia nights, migrating birds and
shimmering fields." The Salesian Missions, by the way, is just a
stone's throw from where I live and from what I hear, it is a
beautiful and serene haven.

For a new and very avid fan, I am happy to enclose an autographed
photo and I'm complimented by the request.

With best wishes,

NANCY TAYLOR ROSENBERG
NTR:im

P.S.My compliments on your very attractive handwriting!

DUTTON • 375 HUDSON STREET • NEW YORK, N.Y. 10014 • FAX: (212) 366 - 2933
DIVISION OF PENGUIN USA

WINGS OF FAITH

Laurel Park
Wappingers Falls, NY
12590

August 3, 1999

Dear Mr. Harrison,

914-462-4214

I had the pleasure of reading one of your poems published by the Salesian Missions. Your poetry is absolutely wonderful. I am the owner of a small, ethnic, Christian card company named Sendjoy. Our mission is to present cards of quality and inspiration. We are not very large but very dedicated. One of my favorite poems is "Your Blessings Are So Many, Lord!". If there is any way that I could discuss with you the possibility of using this poem on a greeting card I would greatly appreciate it.

I can be reached at the above address and phone number or fax 462-4216 and internet address *floydo@vh.net*. I look forward to meeting you in the future. God bless you in your future endeavors.

Sincerely,

Joyce Townsend
President

WINGS OF FAITH

Why Worry About Tomorrow?

Why worry about tomorrow
And the rising of the sun,
Or anguish over past mistakes
That cannot be undone?
Why waste life's precious moments
On things that bruise the heart
When today is ours to fashion
Into a work of art?
Today comes but once, my friend,
It never can return –
So use it wisely while you can,
There's a lesson you may learn.
Let history record the past
And tomorrow come what may.
Be content to do your best
With what you have today!

Clay Harrison

WINGS OF FAITH

Each April, to celebrate National Poetry Month, the Daily Press newspaper sponsors an annual on-line contest: both a Poet Laureate and a Reader's Choice contest. I won the Reader's Choice twice and lost by one vote another time. My winning poems were about the Relay for Life poem for my friend, Naomi, and the Boston Marathon bombing.

WE ARE IN THIS FIGHT TOGETHER

We are in this fight together until a cure is found.
We take the blows and we survive to fight another round.
When the odds are stacked against us, there is no need for tears.
Faith allows us to clear our minds and also calms our fears.
We may be bruised and battered, even knocked to our knees.
It's then our loved ones cheer us on to survive rounds like these.
"Big C's" a fierce opponent...shows no mercy in the ring,
But knowing we are not alone is a powerful thing.
There are thousands in our corner all searching for a cure,
And as long as we keep fighting, a victory is sure!
God works in mysterious ways...His blessings to bestow.
We are in this fight together, winning blow by blow.

WINGS OF FAITH

CHAPTER NINE

BOSTON STRONG

The Ides of March are over, Easter has come and gone
And on this lovely April day we entered the unknown.
Thousands lined the streets of Boston to watch the marathon,
An American tradition that continues on and on.
They came from many nations with dreams all their own
For in the midst of huddled masses, each runner runs alone.
A sudden blast, a cloud of smoke, a shriek, a cry, a moan
Followed by a second blast and precious dreams were gone!
Newlyweds each lost a leg; the winds of war had blown.
An eight year old had lost his life; his sister's leg was gone!
The unimaginable had happened; we entered the unknown.
Evil never takes a holiday but hope lives on and on!

Alzheimer's is one of life's cruelest diseases. It was given national attention when Ronald Reagan succumbed to it, and the book, Tuesdays With Morrie, was made into a movie starring Jack Lemmon.

Quite a few members of our church have had, or lost family members, to this dreaded disease. The most recent case was my neighbor and friend, Duie. When he lost his seven year battle with Alzheimer's, he had become a living skeleton strapped to a board. It began when he couldn't find his way home and couldn't remember his friends' names. It progressed when he didn't recognize his wife or his children and he couldn't remember how to walk from time to time. Inactivity brought weight loss, and in the final stages, he couldn't talk at all.

WINGS OF FAITH

Duie had been a strong, powerful man who was a Staff Sergeant in the Air Force. He delivered Agent Orange during the Vietnam War. In retirement, he was a handyman always ready to help anyone.

Another friend and Olive Branch member who battled Alzheimer's was Retired Lieutenant Commander Murray Moyce. He was a naval officer who once served with Senator John McCain. Murray sang in our choir for years until the onset of this disease. It lasted ten years. In the final stages, he thought his wife was his mother. It broke her heart. Although she was in poor health herself, she prayed to God that she would be allowed to live long enough to take care of Murray. Her prayers were answered.

At Olive Branch we support the annual Alzheimer's Walk fundraiser each year. For several years I participated in the walk but due to a bone spur in my foot, I was unable to continue doing that. I write poems for the event each year.

WHEN LOVED ONES BECOME STRANGERS

When loved ones become strangers, it's an eclipse of the heart
To watch them slowly fade away as their memories depart.
Alzheimer's is a cruel disease – it causes great despair
To look into a loved one's eyes and see no sparkle there.
Month by month, and day by day, they drift farther away
Into a void where we can't go, where they are forced to stay.
Once they pass the point of no return it's difficult to cope
As we pray for a miracle and fiercely cling to hope.
There are many searching for a cure – the battle rages on.
When loved ones become strangers, they never are alone.
God sends them attending angels to guide them on their way,
And we continue to love them as we wipe our tears away.

WINGS OF FAITH

CHAPTER NINE

WHEN YOU LOSE SOMEONE YOU LOVE

When you lose someone you love, tears will surely flow
Remembering all the good times you shared so long ago.
When you lose someone you love, their love abides with you.
Even death cannot destroy or mar the joys that you once knew.

A WORLD OF THEIR OWN

Where do they go when they leave us, the ones we love so much
Who no longer recognize us or respond to our touch?
Does their candle burn at both ends, or has the fire gone out,
When eyes have lost their sparkle, replaced by fears and doubt?
How do we hide the heartaches when our loved ones are lost?
When we don't know how to find them, how great will be the cost?
Our hears must keep on beating, but nothing is the same
When those we've loved forever can't remember our name.
As they slip away, be gentle – be patient and be kind,
For somewhere they are searching for those they left behind.
Surely angels watch over them somewhere in the unknown,
For God wouldn't leave them helpless in a world of their own.

NURSING HOME

Two years in a nursing home made her feel much older.
Every day is like the day before, her world a little colder.
She has only fading memories to keep her company,
And albums of old photographs of people she can't see.
They say these are the "golden years," she can't remember why.
If no one calls again today she'd be content to die.

WINGS OF FAITH

Wisconsin Representatives of Activity Professionals
P.O. Box 1073, Eau Claire, Wisconsin 54702-1073

Dear Sir;

My name is Martha Bechard, ADC – Activity Director who is assisting the Wisconsin Alzheimer's Association plan a training session during their annual conference for professionals in the health care field and caregivers to be held on May 1-3, 2003. During the training session we are going to be holding a breakout where we teach individuals how to make reminisce kits using poems, recipes or articles to stimulate conversation with residents, offer diversion and foremost bring back fond memories. We are asking for permission to use the poem written by you titled Old Things Are More Beautiful which was found in the Ideals magazine – Nostalgia Vol. 44 No. 5 Aug.

If permission can be given or are in need of any further information please contact me;
Martha Bechard
Crystal River Nursing and Rehab Center
1401 Churchill St.
Waupaca, WI. 54981

Phone: 715-258-8131
Fax: 715-258-0179

Thank you so very much for your assistance and look forward to your answer at your convenience.

Sincerely,

Martha Bechard; ADC
Activity Director

A few years ago, Pastor Nickols of Our Saviour's Lutheran Church and Rev. Whitehead of New Zion Baptist Church, began hosting a Senior Champion Program once a week to give caregivers a break. Activities are provided along with lunch and fellowship with other seniors. I volunteer to give poetry readings at both churches each month. I have always had a special place in my heart for seniors and children. I enjoyed the years I spent as a poet in the schools, and now as a volunteer for seniors. At one of my poetry readings to seniors at Our Saviour's, I witnessed firsthand the power of poetry. I was reading an inspirational poem and one of the seniors was paying rapt attention. Suddenly he reached out for the handwritten poem in my hand. He stared at it for a moment and slowly started to read it out loud.

There was a hush in the room as he read. There were tears in the volunteer's eyes. The leader of the program, Joan, squeezed my hand and whispered, "You're witnessing a miracle!" The man reading my poem back to me hadn't spoken a word for two years! There is currently a blind man who attends but doesn't talk much. Every now and then, I get an "Amen!" or "I remember that!" while I am reading.

I wrote a poem for the volunteer's banquet at the Colonial Heritage ballroom called, "Growing Old, But Young At Heart." It ends with this line, "There's a special place in heaven for those who volunteer."

Because God gave me the gift of poetry at an early age, I have made friendships that have lasted a lifetime. Now that I have reached those fabled "Golden Years," I have lost quite a few friends who inspired and encouraged me for decades. There are many I have never met in person who live in other parts of the country. Some write poetry, others just enjoy reading the simple "say what you mean and mean what you say" inspirational poetry that I write. No one needs an interpreter to understand my poems. I don't try to impress people with Mensa-type words.

One of my most enduring long distance friendships is with Kay and Tom Gibson in Watson, Missouri. For almost forty years now, we have exchanged Christmas gifts. When Kay's

WINGS OF FAITH

mother passed away, she used my poem, "Yellow Roses" that I wrote for my mother because they were her mother's favorite flowers too.

Around the time I met Kay through poetry journals in which we both appeared in on a regular basis, I heard a Paul Harvey radio broadcast about a star athlete with a bright future ahead of him who had died suddenly. I wanted to rea out to that family so I wrote them a poem offering hope and comfort. I forwarded it to them through Paul Harvey and we have been corresponding ever since. I send them the Salesian Missions Christmas book every year so they have quite a collection.

Dave and Laura are kind and talented people. He is an excellent painter of landscapes and nature. She uses his paintings to make greeting cards. The card I received this year is lovely. It included a note that the poem I wrote for their son still hangs in their home.

During the 1970's, I was a regular in IDEALS. June Cotner, a publisher in Washington, also uses my poetry in her coffee table books which are sold in book stores and even at Cracker Barrel.

WINGS OF FAITH

I sometimes receive unusual requests forwarded to me by publishers. The strangest came from a lady in Florida who loved my poetry and wanted to marry me! Shirley opened the mail one day and read it to me. Sight unseen, she wanted to marry me. That was the only letter from a reader that went unanswered. Some things can't be explained! A friend of mine discovered that a lady in another state was putting her name on my Salesian poems and selling them to magazines. I contacted the publisher and put a stop to that. While working at Tampa International, a female officer was getting married. She asked me to write a poetic version of her wedding vows, which I did. She invited me to attend her wedding which was being held at a nudist colony. I declined. If there was no place to pin my badge, I wasn't going!

I wrote a poem about food for our church cookbook a few years ago. The publisher thought I must be a woman so I became "May" Harrison in the cookbook. As a police officer, I have certainly been called worse names!

SOMETHING FROM THE KITCHEN

Some of life's most precious moments involve a family meal
When loved ones come together and memories congeal.
Grandma's hand-me-down recipes, Aunt Mary's apple pie,
Remind us of the "good old days" and holidays gone by.
Whether southern-fried or oven-baked, good food's always a treat.
Home cooked meals are a slice of life few frozen foods can beat.
From soul food to a barbeque, from soup to soufflé,
Recipes are the portals to a place called yesterday.
Christmas cookies, spiced gingerbread, are delightful to eat.
Each mouth-watering recipe is a toe-tapping treat.
Recipes recall memories of those no longer there,
The empty chair where grace was said and heads were bowed in prayer.

WINGS OF FAITH

CHAPTER NINE

SWEET DREAMS

When ice cream cost a nickel, I never had a cent
As I dreamed of tutti-frutti and sometimes peppermint.
Times have changed throughout the years and now that I can buy it,
It reduces me to tears because I'M ON A DIET!

On November 22, 2015, while Shirley and I were at Cracker Barrel, everyone seemed to be asking about turkey dinners. It made me think about the reason we celebrate Thanksgiving in America. So, I began to write a poem on my dinner napkin. Our waitress was curious so I showed her the poem when I completed it. She was impressed.

Back at home, I copied the poem on pretty paper and gave the napkin version to our pastor, Richard Cline. He told me that he used it for a devotion when his family gathered for their Thanksgiving dinner.

IT'S NOT ABOUT THE TURKEY

It's not about the turkey, the ham or pumpkin pie,
It's the feeling of Thanksgiving that transforms you and I.
It's not about the things we eat that make us who we are.
It's the joy that comes from blessings God sends from near and far.
It's the love we share with others, the laughter through the tears,
That create the sweetest memories that grow fonder through the years.
It's remembering the loved ones who are no longer there,
Those who nurtured us in childhood days with tender loving care.
Even when we're not together, I'm thankful in my heart
For thoughts and prayers sent my way whenever we're apart.
It's not about the turkey that makes Thanksgiving Day.
It's about the love that we receive and the love we give away.

239

WINGS OF FAITH

Local poets were invited to the Peninsula Fine Arts Center in Newport News to view paintings and create poetry to describe them.

Child's Head

Abbott Handerson Thayer

Life became all but unbearable for Thayer and his wife in the early 1880s, when two of their 5 children died unexpectedly, just one year apart. Devastated, they spent years relocating from place to place.

Perhaps best known for his 'angel' paintings, he used his 3 remaining children, Mary, Gerald, and Gladys as models.

Abbott Handerson Thayer
1849 - 1921

ON VIEWING ABBOTT THAYER'S "CHILD'S HEAD"

She was one of three remaining
for two siblings passed away
And the loss was overwhelming
within her heart that day.

She was a dream awakening
in the summertime of life,
A dream etched with pain and sadness
that cut deeply as a knife.

Her father had lost two children
who departed life too soon
And his sun hid behind a cloud
and darkened his moon.

Now he's sketching her portrait,
one of three who remain
Adding love to every brush stroke
to camouflage his pain.

WINGS OF FAITH

CHAPTER 10

CAT TALES AND OTHER ANIMALS

"And God saw everything that He had made, and behold, it was very good." Genesis 1:31 NIV

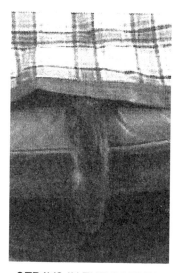

STRAYS IN THE GARDEN

*Twice a day they come our way because they somehow know
That we will give them food and drink and they are free to go.
Some linger in our garden because they have no home,
And they rest among the flowers when there's no need to roam.
They are the walking wounded, these homeless cats we feed,
And somehow they seem to trust us to meet their daily need.
How much like these strays we come to seek our daily bread
In a world filled with strangers who care not if we're fed.
But the Master gives us food and drink because He loves us so
While we linger in His garden with nowhere else to go.*

WINGS OF FAITH

April 16, 1997

_____ *The* _____
NATIONAL HUMANE
EDUCATION SOCIETY
Fostering a sentiment of kindness to animals

Dear Mr. Harrison:

This is to notify you the poem you submitted to The National Humane Education Society, "Strays in the Garden", has made its way into our newest book: *Paws for Thought: How Animals Enrich Our Lives and How We Can Better Care for Them.* The book is a collection of poems and stories that beautifully demonstrate how pets enhance our lives. It is scheduled for publication later this month and distribution beginning in May of this year.

Congratulations are certainly in order, particularly in light of the thousands of pieces of material we receive each year. I assure you a copy of the book will be sent to you before being sent to other members via our direct mail program.

If you have any questions or concerns, please do not hesitate to contact me or my assistant in this project, Mrs. Elisabeth Vlk, at 703-777-8319.

Sincerely,

William J. Kropp
Executive Director

Shirley and I have always been animal lovers. In Tampa, we were feeding up to fifteen cats twice a day. Most of them were strays that came for a meal one day and brought a friend with them the next day. Some slept in shady areas of my gardens. Others, like Genghis Khan, a battle-worn tomcat, came limping down the street twice a day for a meal. No one could touch him. One day he was too wounded to walk away, too close to death to resist when we took him to the vet. He survived and became our favorite house cat. He loved being petted and spoiled rotten as a house pet. When he died years later we all cried and still do sometimes when we think of him.

GENGHIS KHAN-WARRIOR CAT

When we moved to Williamsburg, we brought one cat with us. Simba was a young cat who seemed healthy. Sadly, he came down with feline leukemia shortly after we settled in and he had to be put down. We had him checked by our vet in Tampa but he was too young for the virus to show up at that time.

Our next door neighbor had an outdoor cat named Kitten who was kept outside due to the owner's allergies. She immediately came to our house to be petted and to get treats. When Simba died, Kitten moved right in each time we opened the door and slept with us at night. She would go back home during the day, but it became apparent that she wanted to live with us. The neighbors didn't mind, but they loved telling people we "stole" their cat!

Kitten soon became my lap cat. She would curl up on my chest and snooze for hours if I let her. She would not allow any other cat in our house. About a month before Kitten died after 13 years with us, a cat that could have been Kitten's twin, showed up at our house. She took residence on our front porch and banged on our front door wanting to come in. But Kitten would have no part of that.

243
WINGS OF FAITH

LAP CAT

Kitten comes when it pleases her and sits upon my lap.
She squirms and purrs a little while then takes a little nap.
Kitten may be our neighbor's cat, but she adopted us.
She comes to visit every day and never makes a fuss.
When Simba died and broke our hearts, Miss Kitten bridged the gap.
She brings her love from just next door and lays it in my lap!

Kitten started having mini strokes and we knew her time was growing short. The night she died, Shirley and I held her all throughout the night. She passed away early the next morning. I buried her in our back yard. We finally let the new cat in the house and named her Sammi. She's been with us six years now and has never gone outside. She came to us declawed but had been put out to fend for herself. Sammi is now my lap cat too. Every pet comes with a story, and we could write a book about the pets we have cared for and loved through the years.

We have had a menagerie of pets...puppies and kittens, rabbits, guinea pigs, a parrot, a parakeet named E.T., a descented skunk, two ball pythons, ducks, turtles, a litter of puppies born under our bed, too many cats to count and an iguana that we

WINGS OF FAITH

walked on a tiny leash, to name a few! In Williamsburg we are down to two cats, Sammi and Shadow. They both showed up one day and refused to leave.

Since Sammi followed in Kitten's paw prints as my lap cat, she has adapted quite well to living inside the house. When she first came here, she would come on the run and jump in my lap without looking. It didn't matter if I was eating, writing, or reading a book. I ended up with some nasty scratches.

Little by little, I taught her to approach slowly so I could clear my lap. Once I put my legs up on the hassock, she knows it is safe to jump up. She has since learned to get down when I say, "It's nite-nite time," "I have to go bye-bye," "I'll be back," and "I'll see you in the morning." She grunts and hops down. When our bedroom door opens in the morning, she runs down the hall, hops on the hassock in front of my chair, and waits for a morning back massage. If I'm slow coming down the hall, she "yeows" at me!

On the morning of December 22nd, I had my second skin cancer operation. This one was on my forehead. Every time I rolled over in bed it caused me pain so I spent the night in my recliner working on the manuscript for this book, nodding off now and then. Sammi wanted some lap time so I talked to her about how this was a holy time of the year.

Unlike many cats, Sammi makes intense eye contact with me and it looks like she understands what I'm talking about. So I explained the Christmas story to her, how the God who created both of us sent His Son, Jesus, to earth to ransom us from sin. It may sound crazy, but she "yeowed" now and then as if she understood. It helped me get through the night. If only cats could talk!

245

In the summer of 2014, two new cats appeared in our back yard daily. Neither would come up on the deck to eat so we put food by our tool shed. One was white with a touch of gold and we named him Bandit. He stayed three years but never allowed us to touch him.

The other cat had long hair that was terribly matted. He was in dire need of grooming. It took three months for him to trust us enough to allow us to pet him. We immediately brought him in the house.

Once inside, he was content to stay. He followed Shirley everywhere, like a shadow, and that became his name. We took him to the vet to be groomed where he terrorized large dogs in the waiting room! He forced his way out of his kennel and ran like mad all over the place, ending up in one of the examining rooms where he climbed the blinds all the way to the ceiling!

Once he had been groomed, he was beautiful. When we took him in, we thought he was a girl! He was finally able to groom himself once all that matted fur had been removed. Now that he was going to be a house cat, we also had him neutered and declawed. Sammi did not care to share the house with him so we keep him in our bedroom. He has a great view of our back yard and enjoys watching the birds and squirrels at our feeders. He developed a urinary infection which requires prescription cat food for the rest of his life.

He plays hide-and-seek with Shirley, and sleeps on his own pillow in between us. When our granddaughter, Bella, comes

WINGS OF FAITH

to visit, he loves to play with her. Sammi runs from her so it's no wonder that she tells everyone, "I love Shadow!" I think she enjoys visiting him as much as she enjoys being spoiled by us. Each time she comes here, we get our hugs, and then she says, "I want to see Shadow!"

We have rescued dozens of cats through the years and each one had a different personality, like those in Andrew Lloyd Weber's play, CATS.

SHADOW: A CAT TALE

Shadow must think he's a rooster – he purrs at dawn's first light,
Runs through the blinds and jumps in bed all bushy-tailed and bright.
He was a stray that we took in who would not go away.
He played hide-and-seek in our yard 'til he knew he could stay.
We took him to the vet one day and he put on quite a show.
He climbed the blinds and frightened dogs while running to and fro.
He follows us each place we go so we named him Shadow.
He's quite a sight curled up in bed with his head on his pillow
Cats seem to know where they can go to find a helping hand,
To find someone who will take them in when they're living off the land.
And how like them, God feeds us when we have gone astray,
For by His grace we too are fed and sheltered day by day.

WINGS OF FAITH

Since Shirley and I got married, we've never been without pets. Shirley always had pets growing up but as my family moved often, pets were not an option. While we were going steady, she had a dog named Toby who, according to her mother, was an excellent watchdog! However, Shirley and her father proved this was not the case. One day, while Toby was fast asleep on the screened porch, Shirley's dad sneaked up on him, began shouting, stomping his feet, and clapping his hands. Poor Toby was scared out of his mind. He ran through the house, leaving a trail of excrement behind him all the way. The two of them were hysterical but her mom was livid. She promptly told her husband that he could clean up the mess Toby had made.

Our son, Mark, had two pets that were very special to him. He got a parakeet that he named E.T. after seeing the movie. He was determined to teach it to say "E.T., phone home" but instead he taught it to "rap" against his mirror. E.T. was a beautiful green parakeet and we all loved him dearly. He developed a tumor and it broke Mark's heart when he passed away.

As an adult, Mark had a Great Dane mix named Chops who ate everything within his reach – an entire loaf of bread, wrapper and all, a bag of candy kisses – foil and all, and any food left unattended. As he grew old and a bit overweight, he could no longer climb stairs. He died on Christmas Day while we were there and it broke everyone's heart.

WINGS OF FAITH

CHAPTER TEN

CHOPS

Chops was never "just a dog." He had human qualities
Except when he chased squirrels, and had occasional fleas.
His love was unconditional throughout the passing years.
He was the child they never had and shared their laughs and tears.
He was one hundred pounds of joy waiting at the front door
To hear those familiar footsteps when they came home once more.
He would sometimes get in trouble when left alone all day
For he would eat all the candy they forgot to put away.
Like a child on Christmas morning, Chops was happy as could be.
He wagged his tail and then he died beside the Christmas tree.
Twelve years seem like forever, and sometimes they think he's there
Patiently waiting and watching beside a favorite chair.

WINGS OF FAITH

Our daughter Melanie "adopted" two ball pythons and they lived in large aquariums kept closed with bungee cords. The male, Ferris, was four feet long, gentle and laid back. Akasha was a female who was two feet long and quite aggressive. She went A.W.O.L. for three weeks one time and we discovered she had managed to get into the dropped ceiling and could not get back down. So we moved one tile, put a room divider under it, and she managed to drop down to eat her live mouse in the aquarium. From that time on, there were multiple bungee cords to keep her contained.

One summer we got Melanie a small iguana that she took for walks on a tiny purple leash which amused everyone who saw it. A friend was moving and she asked us to take her descented pet skunk named Shotsie. She had the run of the house during the day and slept in her cage at night.

THE FAMILY PET

It always hurt to lose a pet through time or circumstance.
Such a loss cannot be measured by a momentary glance.
Pets are part of the family, dependable and true.
The love is unconditional they lavish upon you.
They're more than mere companions that share our daily lives
And to lose one leaves a wound that cuts deeper than knives.
They leave behind fond memories etched deeply in the heart.
The bonds we forge throughout the years become a work of art.
Pets see us as we truly are but love us anyway.
They stand by us come what may both pedigree and stray.
It breaks our hearts to watch them die as the years advance.
It always hurt to lose a pet through time or circumstance.

WINGS OF FAITH

From time to time we have kept dogs for church friends while they are on vacation. One of our favorites was a King Cavalier Charles Spaniel named Zoe who was a real beauty. She took to me right away and slept on the floor on my side of the bed, snoring like a freight train! She got too close to our cat Sammi one time and promptly got smacked. She yelped loudly but made sure to keep her distance after that encounter. Fortunately, Sammi is declawed so it only hurt Zoe's pride. Zoe was the runt of the litter and as a result, she had some health issues. Her parents, Bruce and Carole, were distraught when she passed away. They asked if I would come to their house and bury my furry friend in their back yard.

Our friends, Debbie and Jeffrey, had two rescued cocker spaniels named Taz and Faith. Taz was deaf and Faith was blind so they were quite a pair. Jeffrey had to go out of town frequently for medical treatments and we kept the dogs every time. Once, when there was a foot of snow on the ground, I dug a trench around our yard so Faith could follow it when she had

WINGS OF FAITH

to go outside. At night, I slept in my clothes so I could watch over them. Faith and Taz were both junk food junkies and they loved McDonald's cheeseburgers, fries, and vanilla ice cream in a cup. Taz would react every time he saw the Golden Arches when he was riding in a car. Jeffrey and his beloved cocker spaniels have all passed away, but the memories remain.

Growing up on the move as I did, made it almost impossible to own a pet. There was one exception. Dad had one job that lasted almost a year so we rented a house that had a small back yard. Mom took me to an Easter egg hunt at a park in Tampa and I won a baby chick that was dyed pink. Dying chicks was allowed back in those days. Thankfully, it is no longer a practice. I was surprised that I was allowed to keep it and I named it Henny Penny and fell in love with her. I kept her in a cardboard box at night until Dad made a makeshift chicken wire cage for her in the backyard. I rushed home from school every day to feed and play with her. One day, I came home and the cage was empty. Mom swore she got out and ran away but I did not believe it. I searched the neighborhood for my pet and cried myself to sleep that night. Two days later, Mom fixed fried chicken for dinner and I gave her a dirty look. She assured me that it wasn't Henny Penny but I had mixed emotions. She was my only pet until I was married.

252

WINGS OF FAITH

When our friends, Bob and Judy, were on vacation we would go to their house twice a day; Shirley took care of the inside animals and I had barn duty. One of their horses, Red Jet, was the Methuselah of equines. He was approaching thirty-eight years old but was still full of spunk and mischief. One evening while he was in his stall, I opened the gate to leave and he head-butted me from behind. He forced his way out into the barn and took off like an escaped prisoner. I swear he was smiling!

Once I got back on my feet, I took off after him as he was heading down the lane towards freedom. I blocked his path, held up my hands and shouted, "Where do you think you are going?" Believe it or not, he stopped and stared at me as though he thought I was crazy. This allowed me to get a headlock on him around his neck. He had no harness so I held on for dear life and yelled for help but no one heard. I started turning him around toward the barn and slowly, one step at a time, we made our way back to his stall. I was exhausted and my heart was beating wildly.

When Shirley finished at the house she came over to the barn and asked what on earth had happened to me. She was worried that I could have really been hurt but I told her I was more afraid of Judy than I was of Red Jet! I could not imagine having to tell her that I had lost her horse.

Silly me, I thought no one would ever know about Red Jet's "jailbreak" but I was so wrong. Bob and Judy returned home and the next morning when Bob went out to the barn to feed the horse, he saw hoof prints between the house and the barn. He got one of Red Jet's horseshoes that was hanging in the barn and it matched to the prints. I was busted! Later in the morning, Judy called to ask if anything out of the ordinary had

253

WINGS OF FAITH

happened while they were gone. I had to fess up, she and Bob laughed, and confessed that Red Jet had done the same thing to Bob. I breathed a sigh of relief. When Red Jet's companion, Dawn, passed away and was being buried out in the pasture, he screamed and tried to kick his stall door down even though he couldn't see what was happening.

Some animals mate for life and I know they grieve when their mate is gone. Early one morning on my way to Bob and Judy's to take care of their animals; in the middle of the road was a dead squirrel. Another squirrel was sitting up beside it, paws together, as if it were praying. I was the only car on the road so I stopped to remove the dead squirrel once the other one left. It was truly a tender moment. A short time later, Bob and Judy took in two donkeys named Tommy and Jenny hoping they would become companions for Red Jet.

Red Jet   Dawn

Jenny and Tommy

WINGS OF FAITH

CHAPTER TEN

ELEGY FOR RED JET

They're digging your grave as I write this with a heavy heart today
For in a few short hours, they will carry you away.
You lived longer than most expected – thirty-eight years in all,
But soon only fond memories will inhabit your stall.
You brought love and sometimes laughter when you came to Rascals Run,
And it's difficult to say goodbye since your time on earth is done.
You've known joy and you've felt sorrow when Dawn was laid to rest,
Then you shared the barn with donkeys who could sometimes be a pest.
We're so sorry that your cancer was causing so much pain
And you did your best to bear it when you could not complain.
You'll be missed but not forgotten throughout the coming years
For your empty stall was baptized by Bob and Judy's tears!

I have long admired animal conservationalist, Jack Hanna, and watch him on television regularly. From time to time, he and Julie Scardena have appeared at the Williamsburg Busch Gardens and I enjoyed meeting them both. He brings exotic animals with him and sounds the alarm about animals that are endangered. While I was in Panama, I rescued a sloth, saw boa constrictors, anteaters, and a variety of monkeys. We share the planet with these marvelous animals and have a responsibility to protect them. During one of his visits, I gave Jack Hanna a copy of the following poem.

255

WINGS OF FAITH

EXTINCTION IS FOREVER

All God's creatures need our help or they won't survive.
We can't pollute the sea and air and keep them all alive.
We can't hunt into extinction the great ape and the whale,
The elephant and tiger or we will surely fail!
We can't destroy the habitats of creatures great and small
And not diminish wildlife so precious to us all.
What if there were no pandas for children to enjoy?
No manatees or koalas for mankind to destroy?
God's creatures need protection for when we count the cost,
Extinction is forever – another Eden is lost!

WINGS OF FAITH

I have always enjoyed documentaries about wildlife and I feel very sorry for large animals that are confined to cages and offered as sport for big game hunters. At one time, hummingbirds were killed to be adornments on ladies' hats. Elephant legs are severed and made into umbrella stands and their ivory tusks are highly prized. Poaching is still commonplace around the world. It is such a shame that there is a demand for these things.

When we lived in Tampa, we "adopted" a gray wolf at an animal refuge in Waldo, Florida which was staffed by volunteers and funded by donations from animal lovers. It was quite a distance from our home but our children loved to visit all the animals. For several years I also supported the Doris Day Animal Protection League through a monthly donation. They lobbied against animals being used by companies to test their products as well as acts of cruelty being inflicted upon them.

After seeing the movie, "Gorillas In The Mist," the story of Dian Fossey, who was murdered by poachers of the mountain gorillas in Rwanda, I wrote to Sigourney Weaver. She sent me an 8x10 color photograph from the movie along with the following letter. She said making that movie touched her life and she became an advocate to stop the poaching and save the great apes. Many celebrities are animal lovers who have taken on this cause such as Jimmy Stewart, Kim Novak, Tippi Hedren, Brigitte Bardot, and Betty White to name a few.

WINGS OF FAITH

CHAPTER TEN

August 1992

Dear Friend:

Thank you for your kind support of my work. If you particularly enjoyed "Gorillas in the Mist" and would like to find out more about saving the mountain gorillas, you can contact The Digit Fund at 45 Inverness Drive East, Englewood, CO 801112-5480, Tel: (303) 790-2345.

The Digit Fund is a non-profit organization that Dian Fossey started in memory of Digit, her gorilla friend that was brutally slaughtered by poachers. They support Karisoki, the research center, and keep the poacher patrols going. Unlike other wildlife conservation groups, the Digit Fund devotes itself exclusively to protecting and studying the mountain gorilla. Rwanda is presently experiencing grave political problems which seriously threaten the gorillas and their habitat.

For a small tax-deductible contribution, The Digit Fund will send you a quarterly newsletter about these magnificent animals. The newsletter carries several stories on gorillas: how many babies are being born, how many animals have been caught in poacher's traps, etc. The Digit Fund will also send you information on how you may adopt a gorilla! I adopted a female gorilla named Maggie who just gave birth to a son called Rainy Weather! Suggestions and educational programs on the mountain gorillas for your local schools are also available.

Any help you can give us at the Digit Fund will be most appreciated.

Yours truly,

Sigourney Weaver

Sigourney Weaver
Honorary Chairperson
The Digit Fund

Groundhogs are an endangered species where we live now. Farmers think nothing of shooting them if they happen to come near their crops. However, when we visited Ottawa a

WINGS OF FAITH

few years ago on one of our bus trips, we discovered that groundhogs are protected there by law. It is a crime to harm them in any way. They roam freely along sidewalks in the evenings and no one bothers them at all. We have several groundhogs that live beneath our compost heap in the far corner of our backyard. They don't bother anything and we feed them apples and carrots. They also nibble on the bird seed that falls on the ground beneath our bird feeders.

DON'T BLAME IT ON THE GROUNDHOG

Don't blame it on the groundhog because winter didn't end.
It wasn't Punxsutawney Phil that brought this ice and wind.
He didn't cause the snow to drift much higher than before.
He was too busy dreaming of his ladylove next door.
Don't blame it on the groundhog because the snow's so deep.
Phil had no way of knowing while he was fast asleep.
He didn't shut the highways down or cause the schools to close.
He didn't tell the weatherman to forecast record lows.
Don't blame it on the groundhog if spring will be delayed.
For the wrath of Mother Nature might spoil the plans you made.
Don't blame it on the groundhog – it's not as bad as it seems.
Let Phil reset his snooze alarm and lie down to pleasant dreams.

WINGS OF FAITH

CHAPTER 11

DOWN MEMORY LANE

"I thank my God for every remembrance of you." Philippians
1:3 NIV

After we retired, our daughter Melanie, and her husband
Mike, bought our home in Tampa. They started their family
and gave us our first two granddaughters, Chloe and Lily. We
were there when they were born, but we missed a great deal
of their childhood living so far away. Now that everyone has
smart phones and computers, it's easier to keep in touch.

WINGS OF FAITH

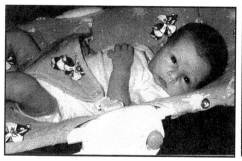 

Chloe Jasmine   Chloe and Lily Belle

DEAR CHLOE AND LILY BELLE

Dear Chloe and Lily Belle, just because I'm not there
As often as I'd like to be, doesn't mean that I don't care.
Because we live in different states nine hundred miles apart,
Doesn't mean that I don't love you and hold you in my heart!
I was there when you were born although you didn't know,
And I'd be there more often if it wasn't so far to go.
Your Mommy sends me pictures and we talk on the phone,
And I'm constantly amazed how much you both have grown.
As you keep growing older, I'm growing older too,
And though my heart is willing, there are things I can't do.
Grandma and I will always love you and hold you close in prayer
So look for us inside your hearts and you will find us there!

They visit us in Williamsburg and experienced their first snow storm here. We are grateful for the Internet so we can keep in touch. Melanie got lots of votes for me each time I won the Reader's Choice Poetry Contest sponsored by the Daily Press. Her pastor asked her to read one of my Christmas poems

WINGS OF FAITH

each Sunday of the 2017 Advent season. Like my friend, Naomi, Christmas is my favorite time of the year, fraught with enduring memories.

Mark and Joy didn't think they could have children, but Isabella Aquino Harrison was born August 15, 2013, and she is beautiful. Since they live less than a three hour drive away, we get to see her quite often. At only four years old, Bella has become a Junior Park Ranger. So far, she has visited every battlefield from Yorktown to Gettysburg and has nearly 150 Junior Ranger badges and patches. Grandma and Grandpa have enjoyed visiting some of these places with her and we are learning along with her.

Bella's current Junior Park Ranger

WINGS OF FAITH

As it is in all of nature, something new is born each day and something old passes away. Shirley and I both lost our parents within a few months of each other. In the summer of 1975, I lost both of my parents. Mom had already survived one open heart surgery to replace a valve, but then it began to fail. The night before her surgery, my blood ran cold as I hugged her before leaving the hospital. In my heart, I knew it would be our final hug this side of heaven. She died on the operating table the next morning. She was only 57 years old.

We had a small service for her in Tampa, and then followed her casket to Tennessee. She wanted to be buried in the family cemetery next to her parents. The fence around the cemetery was covered with white blossoms on blackberry vines. When I went to tell my father that Mom had passed, I learned that he was dying from colon cancer. Uncle Lee came and stayed with us the week before Dad died at age 68. I was sitting by his bed holding his hand when he looked at me and

263

said. "Son, everybody has to go sometime. It's my time to go." He squeezed my hand and he was gone. Dad's new wife, Marguerite, went into a deep depression and passed away on the anniversary of Dad's passing.

Shirley's parents also passed away months apart in 2006. Shirley's mom suffered from COPD and was a petite, frail woman. After breaking her hip, she was bed-ridden and needed constant care. She moved to a nursing home in 2004. Shirley's dad was diagnosed with dementia and joined his wife in the nursing home in 2005. He passed away first at age 92.

We had some comic relief on the way to the cemetery. The elderly driver of the hearse did not follow the lead car. He made a wrong turn and ended up driving through a Target parking lot creating quite a scene. Meanwhile, an anxious crowd was gathered at the graveside wondering what happened to the "guest of honor." When we finally arrived at the cemetery, Mark told everyone that his grandfather, a carpenter, wanted to check out the tools at Target one last time! Shirley's mom was bedridden and could not attend the service. She passed away four months later at age 87 and was buried, without incident, next to her husband of 68 years.

Shirley and I were with her mom the day she died. For hours she stared at the ceiling in the nursing home uttering, "I'm coming, Daddy, I'm coming!" That was her pet name for her husband. This was the first time she had spoken at all in several weeks. One time, she told us her brother, Buster, had come to see her and they had a nice long visit. Suddenly a shocked look came on her face when she remembered that Buster had died many years earlier.

264

WINGS OF FAITH

AMERICANA

Her battlefields are tranquil now across the U.S.A.
Only somber memories remain and ghosts of yesterday.
Bloodstains have long since washed away; cannons no longer roar.
Our unnamed dead in unmarked graves are silent evermore.
From Yorktown to the Alamo, Gettysburg and Bull Run...
From Shiloh to Little Big Horn, the webs of war were spun.
Blood has been shed from coast to coast across the U.S.A.
Our history is etched in blood and haunts us still today.
There's nothing "civil" about war – it's never worth the cost.
Can we ever reconcile the gains with everything we've lost?
We continue to build monuments, lay wreaths, say a prayer
That peace will reign and God will bless Americans everywhere!

WINGS OF FAITH

CHAPTER ELEVEN

One year, our daughter, Melanie, her husband, Mike, and our two granddaughters, Chloe Jasmine and Lily Belle, came to visit for a second time at Christmas. We had assured them that we rarely ever have a white Christmas in Williamsburg. Wrong - we got ten inches while they were here! It started early with gentle snowflakes falling and the girls sitting on our back deck drinking hot chocolate and enjoying it immensely. They had never seen snow before.

Melanie and Mike had a garden wedding on December 26, 1998, in Ft. Myers, Florida. It was so hot that my shoe polish was melting. So you can imagine Melanie's displeasure as snow continued to fall during her visit here. When they left for the hotel, their car was covered with snow. They awakened the next morning to ten inches on the ground! A McDonald's managed to open near the hotel so Mike trudged through ankle-deep snow drifts to get breakfast for his family while the girls made snowmen in the parking lot. They enjoyed every moment, but Melanie vowed she would never again visit us at Christmas time! The family did, however, get to experience snow once more during a visit to New York City. Compared to some hurricanes they have survived in recent years, they discovered a little snowfall wasn't so bad after all.

One year we had a winter storm in Tampa that knocked out power in our area. We spent Christmas at Shirley's parents' home and opened our presents by candlelight. Our children never forgot that Christmas – they still say it was the best one ever. The love we shared being together provided all the warmth we needed.

Mark was diagnosed with CMT, a form of muscular dystrophy, when he was eight years old. That year at Christmas, I was chosen to be the church Santa for our Breakfast with Santa

266

WINGS OF FAITH

program. After the pancake breakfast, the kids lined up to sit on Santa's lap and tell him what they wanted for Christmas. Each child received a gift bag to take home. When Mark sat on my lap, he stared at me and said, "You don't look like my daddy, but you have my daddy's eyes. The doctor said I have dystrophy and all I want for Christmas is not to be sick." My heart was burning as I hugged him, gave him his gift bag, and watched him walk back to Shirley. I couldn't allow the children to see Santa cry. I never played Santa Claus again.

It's amazing how life's most precious memories are made at Christmas time. It truly is a season of miracles and perhaps that is why I have written more poems about Christmas than any other subject. We have a lovely young lady in our church, Maggie Sheppard, who was born with Down's Syndrome and was chosen to be Baby Jesus in our live nativity Christmas Eve Service. Her story was such an inspiration that I wrote a poem for her.

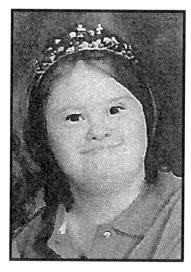

WINGS OF FAITH

CHAPTER ELEVEN

SWEET MIRACLE CHILD

Sweet miracle child, welcome to earth!
Angels in Heaven rejoice at your birth.
God directed your journey, mile after mile,
a bundle of blessings wrapped in a smile.
Some said you're not perfect, but what do they know –
they can't see the soul that touches us so!
God made you a heart from his finest clay;
He filled you with sunshine to brighten each day.
He adorned you with love while you were there,
and sent you to earth in a cradle of prayer.
He sent guardian angels to watch over you,
to a mommy and daddy who cherish you too!
Our hearts have been warmed because of your birth –
sweet miracle child, welcome to earth!
Maggie has grown to love church music.
From her seat in the front pew of the church,
she helps the choir director direct the choir.
It gives all of us an unexpected blessing.

All three of our granddaughters were born by caesarian section. Our son-in-law, Mike, wanted to be in the delivery room for the big event but when there were some complications with Chloe's delivery, he nearly passed out. He was hyperventilating as a nurse rushed him out of the delivery room. When he saw his baby daughter a few minutes later, he was amazed when she lifted her little head upon hearing his voice.

WINGS OF FAITH

When Bella was born, Mark wanted to be present as well. As the incision was made a cyst was nicked and blood spurted in the air. He nearly passed out and again, a nurse stepped in to take charge. He managed to recover and was able to see his daughter being born. Four months later, Bella was chosen to be Baby Jesus at the Christmas Eve Service. Following a quick diaper change on the back pew, she made her debut! She was so sweet and peaceful when she fell asleep in "Mary's" arms that she stole the show! As far as I know, those were the only two times Baby Jesus was a girl at our church.

For the first time in many years, Shirley and I were alone all day on Christmas, except for two curious cats. Our parents are gone now, and our children weren't able to come for Christmas this year. We went to a beautiful Christmas Eve Candlelight Service at Olive Branch, but there was no Baby Jesus this year. We spent the day sorting through hundreds of photos, looking for any to enhance this book. We relived countless memories of Christmases spent as children and those spent with our children when they were young. Memories from back in the "good old days" when toys came with instructions like, "batteries not included" in fine print, and, "some assembly required," which kept me up all night looking for the missing piece someone forgot to include.

Another fun thing was finding hiding places for all the Santa toys a month before Christmas. With the advent of smart phones and Facebook, we are able to exchange greetings with the kids and see what Santa brought this year, as well as what color hair our daughter and her girls have at the moment! Our son-in-law, Mike, shaves his head these days so it makes an interesting family photo with his bald head next to purple, green, or turquoise hair!

269

WINGS OF FAITH

January 4, 2018, brought winter storm Grayson up the east coast. It snowed from Florida to Maine, breaking many records. It also introduced a new terminology to breaking news, "Bomb Cyclone" and nine states had to activate the National Guard. We experienced everything from 75 mph winds, coastal flooding, thunder-snow, single digit temperatures, and dozens of deaths.

January 4th has been a memorable day for our family in the past. Shirley's father died on that date in 2006. A year later on January 4th, Shirley had a mastectomy. On January 4th I was scheduled to have my stitches removed following my second skin cancer surgery. With the snow storm coming, I had them removed one day early.

Remember when doctors made house calls? During my childhood years, when I had measles, mumps, or chicken pox, our local doctor would come to see me at home. There was no "office call" fee and some doctors were kind enough to accept baked goods and a variety of other things as payment. Since my parents never could afford health insurance, I spent many hours in waiting rooms at free clinics.

My current doctor doesn't make house calls but he does go the extra mile. Each time I am waiting for him in the examination room, I hear laughter coming from the adjoining room. He was my neighbor's doctor as well and when Buck passed away, Dr. Seager came to the viewing at the funeral home. He was standing by the casket when I said to him, "Hey, Doc, he told you he was sick!" It added a moment of comic relief, and for once, the joke was on him.

WINGS OF FAITH

MEDICINE FOR THE SOUL

Laughter is a wonderful thing. Medicine for the soul,
For it can give the spirit wings and make the broken whole.
If you can smile when sorrows come then surely you can cope.
When you're wound tighter than a drum, laughter can give you hope.
From time to time, tears may fall upon the bravest cheek.
Times like these can come to all; it doesn't mean you're weak.
When you turn a frown upside down, you'll always feel better
All the world loves a clown in times of stormy weather.
Laughter is a wondrous thing, a treasure to behold,
For the peace and joy it brings is more valuable than gold.
Laughter is a breath of spring when winter takes a toll.
Laughter is a wondrous thing, medicine for the soul.

REMEMBER WHEN

Remember when we sang with Mitch and followed the bouncing ball?
When matinees cost a quarter and there was no shopping mall?
Remember Pop's soda fountain and the local five and dime
Where two could share a sundae and have a real good time?
Remember buying penny candy at the little corner store,
And those old time tent revivals that could last a week or more?
Remember when we did these things not so very long ago,
For now they are the remnants of a life we used to know.

WINGS OF FAITH

CHAPTER ELEVEN

The Wild, Wild West

For Gene Autry's 80th birthday, I wrote him a poem and sent it to him along with a book of my inspirational poetry. I received this letter from him.

5858 SUNSET BOULEVARD • P.O. BOX 710 • LOS ANGELES, CALIFORNIA 90078

September 28, 1992

Dear Mr. Harrison:

I arrived in my office to find your beautiful gift waiting for me, as well as your warm birthday greetings.

Thank you for thinking of me during this time with your kind words, the wonderful book and, most especially your gifted poems. You are very talented indeed.

My best wishes to you always and my appreciate for helping to make my birthday celebration and special time.

Most sincerely,

Gene Autry

WINGS OF FAITH

CHAPTER ELEVEN

One of Gene's friends, another singing cowboy named Fred Scott, discovered my poetry and bought several of my chapbooks. We exchanged many letters in the years to come. When he attended the annual Golden Boot award ceremonies, he would get programs autographed for me and send me photos of western stars who attended. Fred had retired to Palm Springs and wanted to write a book of poetry for his grandchildren. He asked me to edit it for him which I was happy to do, but sadly he passed away before it was completed.

9/23/87

Dear Clay:

Mary and I have read your beautiful book of poetry avidly. We love poetry and write little verses to each other but not of your caliber, I'm sorry to say.

I am enclosing a check for $30.00 with the request that you will send us as many copies as this will buy. We want not only to help Jerry's Kids, but also they will make wonderful presents to mail to a couple of friends I have.

You have a fine talent and we have enjoyed the work so much! My daughter Brenda, dropped by the other day and picked up the book and read it thru at one sitting and said she loved it!

And thanks a million for the the shoulder patch, Far more colorful than my other patches!

Well, thank you again

Fred Scott

FRED AND MARY SCOTT • 1716 Camino Parocela • Palm Springs, CA 92264 • 619-327-9334

WINGS OF FAITH

Fred Scott and Gene Autry 1989   An 87 year old kid with his Golden

Roy Rogers and Fred   Iron Eyes Cody, Lois January, and Fred

WINGS OF FAITH

WHAT HIS EYES HAVE SEEN
(For Iron Eyes Cody)

What his eyes have seen could fill a book, or maybe two or three.
Stories of how the west was won and how things used to be.
His eyes have seen both good and bad across the great frontier
When buffalo herds roamed at will but now he sheds a tear.
His eyes saw the railroads come and settlers from the east
To take the land his fathers owned before they were deceased.
He saw the California gold rush, the dust bowl later on,
And a settlement called Hollywood replaced the land he'd known.
His eyes beheld the "trail of tears," the beginning of the end,
For the Native Americans who vanished with the wind.
He's seen things that make him cry, things nevermore to be.
What his eyes have seen could fill a book, or maybe two or three.

I corresponded for many years with Sunset Carson, whose given name was Mickey Harrison. When he passed away, I wrote a tribute poem for him in a western magazine. I also corresponded with June Storey, who was one of Gene Autry's favorite leading ladies. She wrote poetry while fighting her battle with cancer and we became good friends.

WINGS OF FAITH

JUNE STOREY
P.O. Box 2106
Vista, Calif. 92083

10-26-87

Dear Clay,

Thank you for
your letter and
congratulations not only
as a police officer, but
as a poet w/ unselfish
motives

From time to time
I write a bit too —
enclosed is one I
composed one night
to send to a marine
in radio intelligence
overseas.

Enclosed are some
photos — I will look
forward to your book

Viva Conklin's

June Storey

WINGS OF FAITH

DALE EVANS
Leading lady of Roy Rogers,
on and off screen

JUNE STOREY
Favorite leading lady of Gene Aut...

WINGS OF FAITH

Autographed Dell Comic Books

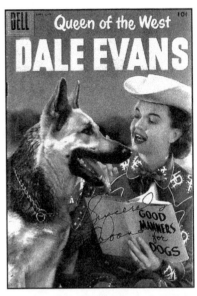

WINGS OF FAITH

CHAPTER ELEVEN

There is a lady in Williamsburg, Cindy Perry, who hosts western festivals and get-togethers at her ranch-style home three times a year. She has hundreds of reels of old western movies which she shows on her projector. Guests bring food to share, and for three Saturdays a year, a room is filled with 70-80 year old buckaroos that are suddenly twelve years old again. For several decades she and her husband brought western actors to town for western film festivals. Sadly, there aren't many of these actors still living. They were among the nicest people I have ever met.

WHATEVER HAPPENED TO...?
(For Cindy Perry)

Whatever happened to Lash LaRue, Red Rider and the rest?
Where are my six gun heroes now who rode the wild, wild west?
Whatever happened to Joel McCrea, Tim Holt and Randolph Scott?
Where are the singing cowboys I really liked a lot?
Whatever happened to Gabby Hayes, Pat Buttram and Fuzzy Knight,
All the comic western sidekicks who'd rather run that fight?
Where are the lovely leading ladies, Dale Evans, Nell O'Day
And alluring Rhonda Fleming...? They all have gone away.
Whatever happened to the "bad guys," Jack Palance, Lee Van Cleef
And Roy's nemesis, Roy Barcroft, who was mean beyond belief?
Tom Mix, Tex Ritter, Eddie Dean, and Alan Rocky Lane...
Cowboys gone but not forgotten because memories remain.

279

WINGS OF FAITH

While watching the funeral of first lady, Barbara Bush, on April 21, 2018, I realized we have something in common. It was pointed out that the three most important things in her life were faith, family and friends and I feel that way too. Without faith, nothing else matters. Christ has been the light unto my path since I was sixteen years old and without Him, I surely would have gone astray and lost my way. By faith I have been blessed beyond measure.

My parents lived and died below the poverty line, but they eked out a living, worked hard, and died young. They made sure that I went to church and lived by the Golden Rule, respected all people, and always told the truth, even when it was painful to do so.

Throughout my spiritual journey I have been blessed with some of the best friends anyone could hope to find. You have been introduced to quite a few of them in this book. I treasure every hug I receive and every prayer said on my behalf. By faith I have survived poverty and racism as a child, 35 years as a soldier and police officer, and a major heart attack. God gave me a wonderful soul mate in Shirley. Our 51 year marriage has flown by like spinning pennies. Our children and granddaughters are our pride and joy.

The gift of poetry has brought me into contact with people from all walks of life for 60 years so far. I write poetry that inspires and encourages people to keep the faith and never quit when the going gets tough. I am blessed each time I read to seniors or enter a classroom where it all began for me in Mrs. Schilling's English class. There are 113 references to faith in the concordance of my King James Bible! If you are a "doubting Thomas," faith the size of a grain of mustard seed

280

WINGS OF FAITH

can move mountains and change your life. Your blessings will multiply when you put your faith into action. I am living proof of that! I wish you well on your spiritual journey. Keep your eye on the prize, and as Mom would say, "always wear clean underwear!"

WINGS OF FAITH

ABOUT THE AUTHOR

CLAY HARRISON has been writing poetry for sixty years, and has been widely published. Nearly two hundred of his poems have been set to music, nine poems have been included in paintings by Danny Hahlbohm, and two were printed on Leanin' Tree greeting cards.

He has written poems for many people and presented poetry programs at schools and for seniors at local churches and nursing homes. You can find his work on the Internet and on You Tube. As Clay would say, "It truly is a wonderful life!"

OTHER BOOKS BY THE AUTHOR

I Am the Clay   Chapbook for MDA
Tomorrow's Angels   Chapbook for MDA

WINGS OF FAITH